WHEN INJUSTICE AND VIOLENCE REIGN

Living a Life of Faith and Hope in A Chaotic World

By

Effie Darlene Barba

Effie Darlene Barba

Published in Columbia Missouri by

Effie de Barba Publishing

P.O. Box 30829

Columbia, MO 65205-3829

(407) 506-5205

© 2017 Effie Darlene Barba

Front Cover Photo

by Permission Oliver Hihn on Unsplash

ALL RIGHTS RESERVED

No part of this publication may be reproduced, stored in a retrieval system, or transmitted, in any form or by any means, electronic, mechanical, photocopying, or otherwise—without prior written permission.

ISBN-13: 978-0-9991193-2-7

Effie Darlene Barba

Unless otherwise noted, scripture is from the King James Version Bible

Also used:

The Living Bible (TLB)
The Living Bible copyright © 1971 by Tyndale House Foundation.
Used by permission of Tyndale House Publishers Inc., Carol Stream,
Illinois 60188. All rights reserved

Effie Darlene Barba

Table of Contents

Chapter 1: Why God? Why Does Injustice and Violence Reign?............1

Chapter 2: One Burdened Prayer and An Unexpected Answer From God..9

Chapter 3: How to Wait for the Answer After Asking God Why..........19

Chapter 4: One Nation Under God Besieged by Evil Within...............27

Chapter 5: In Due Time, Evil Will Be Destroyed..............................35

Chapter 6: How to Recognize the Beginning Sources of Evil.............41

Chapter 7: When Does Trembling Fear Turn to Faith......................53

Chapter 8: God's Glory Revealed in Justice and Mercy....................63

Chapter 9: When Justice Must Reign for Love to Be Complete.........81

Chapter 10: How Can Words of Comfort Really Be an Admonition..89

Chapter 11: How to Know Revival of Faith When All Seems Lost......95

Chapter 12: How to Bring a Revival of Hope When All Seems Lost 105

Chapter 13: When Evil Begins Within, The Walls are Broken How?...113

Chapter 14: An Evil Nation Destroyed by Just Righteousness Why? 121

Chapter 15: Awaken Christians, The Day of the Lord is Near............129

Chapter 16: When Perfect Love and Judgment Meet, Where Are You?...137

Chapter 17: How to Know Love that Overcomes Rejection...............145

Chapter 18: Could We As a Nation Be in Peril of Judgement...........151

Chapter 19: How to Overcome Divisions and Spread the Gospel.....163

Chapter 20: So Dear Lord: What Do We Do Now?........................171

Bibliography..179

Effie Darlene Barba

Chapter 1:
Why God? Why Does Injustice and Violence Reign?

We look around us at the violence raging in the world and ask God why? Why have you not rained down your judgement upon all these evil people? For you are the Almighty, Sovereign God; then, why would you allow so much evil among your own people to occur: the hypocrisy, lies, and immorality? Furthermore God, why do you allow your people to suffer underneath the oppression of evil around the globe? People suffering from earthquakes, floods, hurricanes, cancer, chronic illness, addictions, and personal crisis. Every day, we see the effects of sin upon the lives of all: those who accepted your gospel gift of grace and those who do not. Then where is the answer we seek? Why God, does such injustice and violence reign upon this planet called earth? When will you come down and make it right?

We ask so many questions and there are those moments our faith trembles within. How often have I even narrowed those questions to just my life? Those moments when my own faith trembles or I am pleading, seeking God's will; while my feet still stumble, or my words speak despair into the lives of others instead of light and hope. How does one find hope, joy, love and strength in such a world?

Ah, yes; my hope rests in God's immutable, unchanging face of love and His Mighty Sovereign Hand of Perfect Righteousness and Justice! No matter how dark the road may appear. Regardless of how devastating the storm; God IS the great I am, and He is working all things together for my good and for the good of all who place their faith in Him. This I have learned over a lifetime-the foundation upon which I stand is Jesus Christ. Arising each morning with steadfast joy; I can go boldly before His throne of grace; because He paid the price for my sin. He considered the cost and died for me all the same.

INJUSTICE AND VIOLENCE REIGN

The nation of Israel had a wonderful time of revival and restoration during the reign of Josiah from about 640-609 BC. A great leader, having restored the law and order as well as the true worship of God. Then after his death, the kings to follow were evil. They turned from God to seek their own destinies and lead the people into idolatry once more. The few who remained faithful to God were ostracized for their faith. No one listened or headed the warnings of the faithful, their voices silenced by the crowd. They warned the people that judgement must come if they continued down this destructive road, refusing to turn their worship back to God.

When we look across this great nation of ours, do we not see the same? We see evil and hatred in our streets from the White Supremacy to the Anti-FA groups. From main stream media to the streets of Hollywood, hate spews forth against the Christians. Then there are groups such as Black Lives Matter which further divide rather than heal; because of their own racist, hate filled rhetoric. Certainly, I agree that the Black in our nation have been mistreated. We must do more to heal those divides; yet, hating all whites for their color is merely another form of racism and only widens the divide. We cannot survive as a nation if lawlessness and anarchy reign within our streets. Martin Luther King is quoted as saying,

> *Darkness cannot drive out darkness; only light can do that. Hate cannot drive out hate; only love can do that…We have before us the Glorious opportunity to inject a new dimension of love into the veins of our civilization.* [1]

Respectful dialogue, lawful order must be restored with love and kindness our vehicle to heal this nation. But the wounds are deep, and it will require dedication and

---

[1] Dr. Martin Luther King, Jr, "Martin Luther King Quotes," Movingtowardfreedom.com, accessed 11/4/2017, https://movingtowardsfreedom.com/tag/martin-luther-king-jr-quotes/ (King n.d.)

willingness for every person to set aside their pride. Then with humility and grace we can work to heal those wounds.

Furthermore, when we look around the world, do we not tremble with fear at all the evil surrounding us? There are the Isis terrorists, the North Korean regime, and so many evil plans and plots for war. We see Christians martyred around the world.

WHERE IS HOPE WHEN INJUSTICE AND VIOLENCE REIGN?

We can trust an Almighty Sovereign God who never changes! Let me walk you through the pages of history. We will step back in time and look at three small books in the Old Testament. They are Nahum, Habakkuk, and Zephaniah.

All three of these prophets lived during the time surrounding Josiah's reign with some very specific prophecies. Nahum, the "comforter" told of the fall of Nineveh in Assyria; that God's people might be freed from such tyrannical rule:

portraying God's justice in the world and His mighty power to protect those who know Him. Habakkuk was filled with questions as He foretold of Babylon's rising power to overthrow and take captive the people of Judea. Yet, God would then restore His people; when, the mighty Babylonian kingdom would fall. Zephaniah wrote of God's love amid the storms of life. They each present a part of God's character from His justice to His righteousness and His Love through it all. Let us begin with Habakkuk first, as he was the prophet who questioned God the most with the question, "Why?"

THOUGHTS TO CONSIDER

Faith grows as we learn to see God in all the aspects of His Glory equally. His perfect Righteousness and His Justice are as much of part of who God IS as His Love, Grace and Mercy. Indeed, they are a part of His Love toward us. If God could ignore our sin, demanding no justice for the evil around us; how could that be love? Knowing that the cancer would destroy us, would we protest when God chooses to cut the cancer out or our hearts. Were God unable or unwilling to wield the surgeon's knife, cutting out the cancers of pride or selfishness lurking within our hearts, would that be more loving?

In my previous book, *Abiding, Steadfast Joy*, I wrote about the three foundations of truth upon which we can anchor our faith. The purpose of this book is to look closer at God, Himself: His Just nature, His righteousness, His Love and His Mercy toward the faithful. Also, through a study of Nahum, Habakkuk and Zephaniah we get a glance into how God deals with Governments.

HEBREWS 6: 17-20 (TLB)

> *God also bound himself with an oath, so that those he promised to help would be perfectly sure and never need to wonder whether he might change his plans. He has given us both his promise and his oath, two things we can completely count on, for it is impossible for*

God to tell a lie. Now all those who flee to him to save them can take new courage when they hear such assurances from God; now they can know without doubt that he will give them the salvation he has promised them.

This certain hope of being saved is a strong and trustworthy anchor for our souls, connecting us with God himself behind the sacred curtains of heaven, where Christ has gone ahead to plead for us from his position as our High Priest,

Chapter 2

ONE BURDENED PRAYER AND AN UNEXPECTED ANSWER FROM GOD

There had been a wonderful period of revival during the reign of Josiah. However, his sons did not carry on what their father had begun. Instead, they allowed sin, idolatry, and lust to grow within their hearts and within the hearts of the people they governed. Habakkuk looked around him and saw that people's hearts had turned away from God and his heart was heavily burdened.

When you look around you, are you burdened to see that The Ten Commandments are being removed from the courthouses? Or that prayer is being banned in the schools? Even the appearance of a coach bowing on the 50-yard line, alone in prayer, causes outrage! When we see the breakdown of marriage, the legalization of yet another mind-altering substance in a sea of drug related deaths, and the violence in our streets; are we burdened?

"O Lord, how long shall I cry, and thou wilt not hear!" (Habakkuk 1:2).

Burdened by all you see happening in our land, have you cried out to God? Does it seem that He is silent; while the far-left agenda violently attempt to stomp out religious freedoms or the far right White Supremacy rhetoric of hate grows? God is not; and has never been, silent in the affairs of government. He wasn't in the Old Testament and He is not now! All too often, we mistake His patience for silence; yet, He has a plan and He will complete it. "For the earth shall be filled with the knowledge of the Glory of the Lord" (Habakkuk 2:14).

ONE BURDENED PRAYER/ UNEXPECTED ANSWER

As Habakkuk begins his prayer time with God, he is heavily burdened by all the strife, contention, violence, and self-exalting behaviors within his nation. He cries out to God for allowing such injustice and lawlessness; while the remnant of true believers and worshippers of God are being pushed around by the "wicked." He asks God: "Why aren't you doing something?" (paraphrase of Habakkuk 1:2-4).

God replies; "Wait and see as I am about to do something you will not believe, unless you see it with your own eyes. I am strengthening a very evil nation who will take captive the nation of Judah."

Don't believe me? Read:

HABAKKUK 1:5-9 (TLB)

> *The Lord replied: "Look, and be amazed! You will be astounded at what I am about to do! For I am going to do something in your own lifetime that you will have to see to believe. I am raising a new force on the world scene, the Chaldeans, a cruel and violent*

> nation who will march across the world and conquer it. They are notorious for their cruelty. They do as they like, and no one can interfere. Their horses are swifter than leopards. They are a fierce people, more fierce than wolves at dusk. Their cavalry move proudly forward from a distant land; like eagles they come swooping down to pounce upon their prey. All opposition melts away before the terror of their presence. They collect captives like sand.

FROM BURDENED TO HORRIFIED

Well, if you think Habakkuk was burdened before; now, he is horrified. How could God use evil to combat evil?

> *Art thou not from everlasting, O LORD my God, mine Holy One? we shall not die. O LORD, thou hast ordained them for judgment; and, O mighty God, thou hast*

established them for correction. Thou art of purer eyes than to behold evil, and canst not look on iniquity: wherefore lookest thou upon them that deal treacherously, and holdest thy tongue when the wicked devoureth the man that is more righteous than he? (Habakkuk 1:12-13).

In other words, wait a minute, God! Aren't you perfect righteousness? How can you possibly allow such evil to grow upon the earth? After all, those people I was complaining about. Well, they aren't so terribly evil; like the ones you are going to allow to overthrow us are?

"This was Habakkuk's problem: since the Babylonians were even more wicked than the people of Judah, why would God choose a more wicked nation to punish a nation which was comparatively less wicked? This would not be the first time God had used such a method. In Isaiah 10:5 the Assyrian is called the rod of God's anger...After God had used Assyria for the chastisement of Israel, He judged Assyria for her own sins."[2]

GOD IS SOVEREIGN AND RULES OVER NATIONS

We must be diligently in prayer for our nation, trusting God has a plan that is good for all who seek Him. Does God cause evil to arise? God cannot create evil; however, as He is All that is pure and good; all He must do for evil to rise is steady His hand of judgement and suspend His Presence for a moment in time—evil will rise.

Yet, even then; He does it with a watchful eye; using their evil for our good. As Joseph learned when his brothers, desiring his death; sold him into slavery. Years later, when Joseph sat in a seat of power; his brothers were afraid for all

---

[2] J. Vernon McGee, *Through the Bible with J. Vernon McGee: volume III Proverbs-Malachi,* (Nashville, TN: Thomas Nelson, 1982), 841 (McGee 1982)

they had done. Joseph told them, *"And Joseph said unto them, Fear not: for am I in the place of God? But as for you, ye thought evil against me; but God meant it unto good"* (Genesis 50:19-20).

The same remains true today. No matter how dark the place you are in; God has a plan of good for you if you know Him. Do you know Jesus as your Savior? Do you seek God and to sit in His presence?

GOD'S PROMISES ARE POWER TO RISE WHEN WE ARE BURDENED

That is His promise to us. Yet, He knows that our hearts cannot be satisfied until we find our satisfaction in Him. He is the Joy, the Hope, and the Peace we so desperately need. When you don't see the answers unfolding as you feel they should; remember, and hold fast to God's promises. When this is hard to do, "Stop, remember, He is God and You are not" as was sang in the Song *Thy Will Be Done* by Hillary Scott.

Effie Darlene Barba

It's hard to count it all joy

Distracted by the noise

Just trying to make sense

Of all your promises

Sometimes I gotta stop

Remember that you're God

And I am not

So

Thy will be done

Thy will be done

Thy will be done[3]

---

[3] Hillary Scott, Emily Weisband and Bernie Herms, *Thy Will Be Done*, 2016 W.B.M. Music Corp., accessed 9/25/17, http://www.air1.com/music/artists/hillary-scott/songs/thy-will-lyrics.aspx (Scott and Emily Weisband 2016)

REMEMBER THIS

Faith is knowing God IS (Sovereign, Almighty, Perfect Righteousness, Omnipotent, LOVE, Grace, Perfect Justice—the Great I AM, the Being without whom there is nothingness) and that He rewards those who diligently seek Him. (my paraphrase of Hebrews 11:6)

Effie Darlene Barba

Chapter 3:

How to Wait for The Answer After Asking God Why?

Habakkuk had come to plead for his nation. He first asked God, "Why God haven't you judge the evil within the nation." Wanting righteousness restored, he cried "God, do something!" Yet, God's answer horrified Habakkuk; at least, at first. He turned his question to ask God why once more. This time, his confusion was how God could allow an idolatrous nation such as Babylon to flourish, grow and be given the power to take all of Judah captive. After all, Habakkuk's prayer to revive the nation and cleanse it from so much evil, certainly did not expect God's answer to be "a truly evil power will take everyone captive." Habakkuk, again asked God why. Then, he waits for God's Answer, demonstrating how to wait for God's reply, whether regarding personal, family or national requests of God. How to wait for God's answer when our question is "Why?"

> *"I will stand upon my watch, and set me upon the tower, and will watch to see what he will say unto me, and what I shall answer when I am reproved"* (Habakkuk 2:1).

Watchfully wait for God to show the truth of his reasoning. Many times, in my own life, I searched for God to answer. Asking for God to heal my husband or my mother. I asked God why He allowed the abuse I suffered or the cancer I battled. Why, God, so many surgeries or suffering moments? How can THIS be your plan God? Or perhaps the hardest, why God does it seem that evil is winning?

WATCHFULLY WAIT, EXPECTING AN ANSWER

Habakkuk, after asking why, decided to watchfully wait for God's answer, *"and what I shall answer when I am reproved."* He knew God had a reason, even if he did not understand that reason. He also knew God's reason was just and righteous. That is faith. Even when we cannot see the answer, we know God has a plan for good; because, we know God.

> *For I know the thoughts that I think toward you, saith the LORD, thoughts of peace, and not of evil, to give you an expected end. Then shall ye call upon me, and ye shall go and pray unto me, and I will hearken unto you. And ye shall seek me, and find me, when ye shall search for me with all your heart. (Jeremiah 29:11-13).*

Habakkuk knew that his erroneous misunderstanding of the plan **needed correction**; because, he knew God and trusted that His plan would be best no matter what!

Charles Stanley wrote, "Some of life's greatest lessons are learned while we wait. Some of life's hardest classrooms are waiting rooms. But there are vast rewards in waiting."[4]

---

[4] Charles Stanley, *Charles Stanley's Handbook for Christian Living*, (Nashville, TN: Thomas Nelson Publishers, 1996), 334

(Stanley 1996)

Habakkuk sat aside a place and time to await God's answer to why? He expected that God would answer within the perfect timing of God. Do you have a place and time you meet with God, so He can answer you?

Jerry Falwell lived by faith, often awaiting God's answer to some very profound visions as God called him to establish Thomas Road Baptist Church and to build Liberty University. He claimed that mountain, Liberty Mountain, for God. He wrote, "Spend time with God to get your vision from Him …. The prophet (Habakkuk) had a place and time where he met God."[5]

ANSWER FROM GOD

"And the LORD answered me, and said, Write the vision, and make it plain upon tables, that he may run that readeth it. For the vision is yet

---

[5] Jerry Falwell, *Building Dynamic Faith,* (Nashville, TN: Thomas Nelson Publishers, 2005), 30

for an appointed time, but at the end it shall speak, and not lie: though it tarry, wait for it; because it will surely come, it will not tarry" (Habakkuk 2:2-3).

Don't miss this! As Habakkuk waited, God answered. He told him to write it down clearly, plainly on tablets; so, others see it and read it. Thereby, strengthening their faith through it; because, amid the judgement of the nation that was coming, God had a plan of love for those who would believe. Not everyone in the nation had forsaken God. Only their voices had been silenced. It would be necessary to cleanse the nation of evil; before, all were drawn into darkness. God's answer was a vision of what was yet to come, and the remnant of true believers would need to hold fast to God's promise, by faith as the days would grow darker before the dawn. They would need to hold tight to God's promise, so write it down!

Write down God's promises, cling to them during the storms of this life. They will be the anchor for your soul.

Knowing who God is, we can trust in His plan; even when all appears lost!

WAIT, TRUSTING GOD'S FUTURE GRACE

God told Habakkuk "the vision" WILL happen at a specific God appointed time. Then, He adds, "*Behold, his soul which is lifted up is not upright in him: but the just shall live by his faith*" (Habakkuk 2:4). The redeemed live by faith; not the works of their own hands. "*For by grace are ye saved through faith; and that not of yourselves: it is the gift of God*" (Ephesians 2:8).

THEREFORE, HOW TO WAIT FOR GOD'S ANSWER

1. Watchfully, expectantly, knowing God will answer at His perfect time. Take time to be alone with Him, so you can clearly hear His answer

2. Write down His answer, keep a journal

3. Know that He is present, building your faith as He prepares to bring you His best

4. Rest upon His promises, found in the scripture

5. Never forget, GOD IS THE GREAT I AM AND HE REWARDS THOSE WHO DILIGENTLY SEEK HIM. Are you seeking Him? If so, why worry or fret? He has a perfect plan of love for you.

Although, not all had sinned and turned their back on God. Yet, God knew the remnant of faithful believers could not survive; if He did not cleanse their land of evil. It was an act of love that caused Him to allow this evil to occur. An act of perfect love, that those who by faith trusted in Him; would be able to bask in His joy. Yet, a little while; and their joy would be fulfilled.

Effie Darlene Barba

Chapter 4:

One Nation Under God Besieged by Evil Within

Habakkuk's discourse with God began with a concern for all the evil within the nation of Judah. Violence, Lawlessness, Disrespect toward their heritage, Immorality, and Idolatry were growing rampant in their society. His first question was why God stood silent and allowed such evil within the nation to grow. When God replied that He would allow a greater evil, Babylon to take His people captive; Habakkuk was horrified at first.

How could God use a greater evil to be the source to destroy the evil within the nation of Israel? Yet, Habakkuk knew that God was just. His righteousness and mercy would reign, so; prayerfully and watchfully Habakkuk waited for God's reply. That is where we left off the story last time. Waiting for God to answer. Yet, shouldn't we, the people of the United States of America not also be crying out for our nation?

On June 25, 1962, the United States Supreme Court decided in Engel v. Vitale that a prayer approved by the New York Board of Regents for use in schools violated the First Amendment because it represented establishment of religion.[6] Since then, that decision has been extended to ban any prayers voluntary or not from being used within the schools.

Furthermore, it at times is used to ban children from even carrying a Bible or teachers to pray. Some, if not most schools have stopped the pledge of allegiance to the American Flag. The First Amendment was never meant to keep Faith or Religion out of Government: it was meant to keep Government out of religion. We have sat idly by and watched

---

[6] Penny Starr, "Education Expert: Removing Bible, Prayer from Schools Has Caused a Decline", *CNS NEWS.COM*, August 15, 2014, accessed September 29, 2017, https://www.cnsnews.com/news/article/penny-starr/education-expert-removing-bible-prayer-public-schools-has-caused-decline (Starr 2014)

as Government intrudes further and further into our religious freedoms throughout the years.

ONE NATION UNDER GOD BESIEGED

Since then, we have seen within our schools a steady demise. As Charles Stanley wrote:

> "while Bible and prayer were still in the school system (and seminaries), these were the major problems in school: (talking in class, (2) chewing gum, (3) making noise, (4) running in the halls, (5) getting out of line, (6) wearing improper clothing, and (7) missing the wastebasket. Today these are our problems: (1) drug abuse, (2) suicide, (3) alcohol, (4) pregnancy, (5) rape, (6) murder, and (7) assault."[7]

---

[7] Stanley, *Handbook Christian Living*, 99

This is merely one small piece of a much larger demise within our nation; but, it began in 1962 with one Supreme Court decision. We cannot help but note the change that has overtaken our education system since then, leading to students never hearing even the truth of our own heritage and history. It began a breakdown, which we see all too clearly now. Disrespect of our flag, our heritage, our laws, and our people have grown; because of one decision, which has been used to silence the Christians of this nation regarding education. The decision was never meant to say, individuals could not read their Bible or pray silently in school. Yet, that is what it has been used to do.

No longer are our children taught about the battles won against slavery, against Nazi oppression, against fascism and against segregation as One Nation Under God. Now we have young people growing up never realizing how far we have come because of God being our strength. Instead, we are raising a nation of young people who burn the flag, who transform protests into violent riots and who want to hear nothing about the great strides we have made as a nation and as a people.

> "Today our universities have become strongholds of atheism and secularism. Our science, our art, and our laws are being used to marginalize and discredit the Christian faith. And America, founded on belief in an omniscient, omnipotent Creator, has banished God from every aspect of public life. Western civilization is being undermined from within, like a once-great edifice now being slowly but steadily consumed by termites"[8] Michael Youssef

---

[8] ³Michael Youssef, *The Barbarians are Here,* (Franklin, TN: Worthy Publishing, 2017), 125 (Youssef 2017)

Effie Darlene Barba

BESIEGED BY EVIL WITHIN

The problem continues to grow. "Evil does not stand still—it always progresses toward greater and greater evil."[9] We have continued down some horrid slippery slope. So, what is our only hope? We must like Habakkuk cry out to God first! We must stand upon our watchtower and wait for His answer. Then, we must write that answer upon tablets and carry it to the people.

> "I want us to look primarily at the government of the United States of America because we are leaders in the world. We were leaders in military might, leaders in strong moral fiber, leaders in affluence, leaders in sending the most missionaries out. We are still leaders. Leaders in crime. Leaders in drugs. Leaders in teen pregnancies. Leaders in illiteracy.

---

[9] Youssef, *Barbarians,* 123

Leaders in pornography. Leaders in debt. And fast losing in our preeminence of sending for missionaries"[10] Charles Stanley.

HOPE REMAINS

Babylon did make Israel their captives, enslaving the people. After that, Babylon fell and Israel did stand as a nation once more. Ultimately, *"the earth will be filled with the knowledge of the glory of the Lord . . .the Lord is in his holy temple: let all the earth keep silence before him"* (Habakkuk 2:14,20).

Overtaken by evil from within, the United States of America is running fast toward captivity by extreme ideologies that breed anger, violence, and divide; because, we forsook our first love. However, the followers of Christ know: God

---

[10] [5] Stanley, *Christian Living,* 96

has won the ultimate victory. The road may appear rough at times; yet, we must stand united in prayer, watchful for God's reply. We must take a stand for God and be willing to testify for the name of Jesus Christ. Our mission: is to tell the world of the gospel story. We must begin here at home.

Chapter 5:

In Due Time, Evil Will Be Destroyed

As Habakkuk waited upon his watchtower, longing for God's response; he knew that seeing all the evil within his nation and the even greater evil invading his nation, only God could help him to understand the chaos surrounding his own heart.

We cry for all those injured and killed October 1, 2017 in Las Vegas, as I was writing this page. My own heart wrenching in pain, praying that each soul who perished in the awful event might have known the Savior. Aching from the thought that any should perish without having heard and accepted the gospel message, I like Habakkuk; must stand and wait upon the watchtower to hear God's call. He promises in verses 2,3, and 14 of Habakkuk 2, that in due time, evil will be destroyed.

Effie Darlene Barba

IN DUE TIME:

> *For the vision is yet for an appointed time, but at the end it shall speak, and not lie: though it tarry, wait for it; because it will surely come, it will not tarry. Behold, his soul which is lifted up is not upright in him: but the just shall live by his faith. For the earth shall be filled with the knowledge of the glory of the LORD, as the waters cover the sea.* (Habakkuk 2:3-4,14)

In due time, Christ came to this earth, born of a virgin to die upon a cruel cross. He paid the penalty for mankind's sin; then, on the third day He rose from the grave, conquering sin and death with one great and mighty blow for all who will accept His gift of salvation by believing on the name of the Lord Jesus Christ!

There will come another day when Christ will return. That day is described by Isaiah the prophet,

And he will destroy in this mountain the face of the covering cast over all people, and the vail that is spread over all nations. He will swallow up death in victory; and the Lord GOD will wipe away tears from off all faces; and the rebuke of his people shall he take away from off all the earth: for the LORD hath spoken it. And it shall be said in that day, Lo, this is our God; we have waited for him, and he will save us: this is the LORD; we have waited for him, we will be glad and rejoice in his salvation. (Isaiah 25: 7-9)

EVIL WILL BE DESTROYED

Then cometh the end, when he shall have delivered up the kingdom to God, even the Father; when he shall have put down all rule and all authority and power. For he must reign, till he hath put all enemies under his feet. The

> *last enemy that shall be destroyed is death.* (1 Corinthians 15: 24-26).

When God answered Habakkuk, He told him of a nearer prophecy that one-day Babylon would be overthrown, and Judah would again be freed from captivity; at least, the remnant of believers. Although, God allowed evil forces to take them captive; because of the idolatry of many within their nation. He would restore the faithful to their land in due time.

However, God also spoke of a future time in which Christ would come to pay the price that mankind might be saved. Furthermore, He told of a day yet to come as described by Paul in

I Corinthians 15: 52-58

> *In a moment, in the twinkling of an eye, at the last trump: for the trumpet shall sound, and the dead shall be raised incorruptible, and we shall be changed. For this corruptible must put*

on incorruption, and this mortal must put on immortality. So when this corruptible shall have put on incorruption, and this mortal shall have put on immortality, then shall be brought to pass the saying that is written, Death is swallowed up in victory. O death, where is thy sting? O grave, where is thy victory? The sting of death is sin; and the strength of sin is the law. But thanks be to God, which giveth us the victory through our Lord Jesus Christ. Therefore, my beloved brethren, be ye steadfast, unmovable, always abounding in the work of the Lord, forasmuch as ye know that your labour is not in vain in the Lord.

CONCLUDING THOUGHTS

As we look around us and see so much evil within our nation and around the world, where is our hope? Our hope is in God and His promises! Just as He restored the nation of Israel in Old Testament, He will complete His promises for today, and into eternity.

> *For I know the thoughts that I think toward you, saith the LORD, thoughts of peace, and not of evil, to give you an expected end. Then shall ye call upon me, and ye shall go and pray unto me, and I will hearken unto you. And ye shall seek me, and find me, when ye shall search for me with all your heart.* (Jeremiah 29: 11-13)

So, my question for you is: "Are you seeking Him today?" If so, you will find Him; because, He will make Himself known to you! He promised just that, and He always keeps His promises. Jesus Christ will return one day to establish His kingdom. Evil will be destroyed. No matter how dark it may appear until day, we can rest assured; He is coming again.

Chapter 6:

How to Recognize the Beginning Sources of Evil

The book of Habakkuk begins with a very heavy burdened, saddened prophet. He looks around at his people, the tribe of Judah were the last who were standing with some hope of holding fast to their faith. But, alas; they too had turned from God. Despite the great revival lead by King Josiah; once more, evil, strife, bitterness, greed and idolatry reigned throughout the land.

As shown in the previous chapters; when Habakkuk prayed, He asked God why? Why did you allow this? As though God in His Sovereignty would deny mankind the freedom of choice! However, the price of such freedom comes heavy, when the people choose evil. Did they choose evil because they hated good? I daresay that as always evil begins with pride, covetousness, lustful desires, and a turning away from God to seek after other idols.

That was what happened to the nation of Judah. Although, God declared that an even more evil nation would overtake them; that nation too would fall because of the same evil within. Matthew Henry in his commentary of Habakkuk 2:5-14 wrote:

> "The prophet reads the doom of all proud and oppressive powers that bear hard upon God's people. The lusts of the flesh, the lust of the eye, and the pride of life, are the entangling snares of men; and we find him that led Israel captive, himself led captive by each of these."[11]

Where does evil begin in the hearts of men and women? Is it not always lurking there?

---

[11] Matthew Henry, "Matthew Henry Commentary: Habakkuk 2:5-14," *biblehub,* accessed October 4, 2017, http://biblehub.com/habakkuk/2-5.htm (Henry n.d.)

BEGINNING SOURCE OF ALL EVIL

Evil always has its beginning in pride within the hearts of individuals. Was that not the downfall of Satan, himself? Read of the Bibles description of his fall from heaven.

> *"You were perfect in all you did from the day you were created until that time when wrong was found in you. Your great wealth filled you with internal turmoil, and you sinned. Therefore, I cast you out of the mountain of God like a common sinner. I destroyed you, O Guardian Angel, from the midst of the stones of fire. Your heart was filled with pride because of all your beauty; you corrupted your wisdom for the sake of your splendor.*
>
> *Therefore, I have cast you down to the ground and exposed you helpless before the curious gaze of kings. You defiled your holiness with lust for gain; therefore, I brought forth fire*

> *from your own actions and let it burn you to ashes upon the earth in the sight of all those watching you. All who know you are appalled at your fate; you are an example of horror; you are destroyed forever"* (Ezekiel 28: 15-19 TLB).

And such was the beginning of evil within Satan's heart of pride where covetousness, lustful desires, and idolatry began. Although, we are foretold of the end as well in this passage.

THE BEGINNING AND THE ULTIMATE END OF EVIL

> *How you are fallen from heaven, O Lucifer, son of the morning! How you are cut down to the ground—mighty though you were against the nations of the world. For you said to yourself, "I will ascend to heaven and rule the angels. I will take the highest throne. I will*

preside on the Mount of Assembly far away in the north. I will climb to the highest heavens and be like the Most High." But instead, you will be brought down to the pit of hell, down to its lowest depths. Everyone there will stare at you and ask, "Can this be the one who shook the earth and the kingdoms of the world? Can this be the one who destroyed the world and made it into a shambles, who demolished its greatest cities and had no mercy on his prisoners?" (Isaiah 14: 12-17 TLB).

Since then, Satan draws the hearts of men and women to him by the same means. Was that not the appeal he made to Eve and Adam, leading them to desire the forbidden fruit of the tree of good and evil? He suggested they could be like God; if only they ate? Wouldn't a loving God give you all your heart's desire? (Genesis 3:1-6 paraphrased) Now, since sin entered the world; we are born with hearts bent toward sin. Our only hope is to accept the atoning sacrificial gift of salvation that God has provided. *"The just shall live by faith!"* (Habakkuk 2:4).

WHAT ABOUT AMERICA? HOW ARE WE BREEDING SUCH EVIL?

Is it not selfish pride within the hearts of individuals that breeds such evil? National pride is different, if we hold fast to the principles on which we were founded. When we as a nation, remember that we were founded on the principle.

> "We the people of the United States, in order to form a more perfect union, establish justice, insure domestic tranquility, provide for the common defense, promote the general welfare, and secure the blessings of liberty to ourselves and our posterity, do ordain and establish this Constitution for the United States of America."

Combine that with the preamble to the Declaration of Independence

> We hold these truths to be self-evident, that all men are created equal, that they are endowed by their Creator with certain unalienable Rights, that among these are Life, Liberty and the pursuit of Happiness. **Preamble to the Declaration of Independence**

When we forget that faith in God was a cornerstone principle upon which our nation was founded, or that part of the principle elements of government are to "establish justice and insure domestic tranquility"; then, we allow evil to enter our nation. We must consider the ultimate consequences of our promotion of self-aggrandizement of individuals.

When we sit idly by while our nation murders babies before they are born in the name of "women's rights", or people's protests extend to calling for the death of cops (the very ones who establish justice and insure domestic tranquility), or sit quietly when our freedom to worship God where ever we are is being squelched; then, we should not be surprised as evil grows within the nation we live.

JOHN PIPER WROTE CONCERNING EVIL

Those who resist God are "storing up wrath for themselves on the day of wrath when God's righteous judgment will be revealed (Romans 2:5). On that day it will appear clearly to all how utterly naïve it was for millions of people to live their lives as though the God who made this world for his glory would never call them to account for how little he has meant to them. It squares with Scripture, and it squares with reason: "He has fixed a day on which he will judge the world in righteousness" (Acts 17:31), Therefore, I urge you to ask yourself: Would I gain my life before a holy God if I died tonight? Am I ready to take my stand in the divine courtroom and hear the Judge pass an eternal sentence on me? There will only be two verdicts in that day, and one or the other of them will be passed on every person: either "condemned" or "justified," hell or heaven, eternal death or eternal life

Habakkuk taught us that when judgment comes the just shall live by his faith. And when that seed comes to full flower in the New Testament, we see that the reason the just live by faith is that the just are justified by faith. As Paul puts it (and with this invitation I close), "They are justified by his grace as a gift, through the redemption which is in Christ Jesus, whom God put forward as an expiation by his blood, to be received by faith" (Romans 3:24).[12]

GOD's Word:

There is therefore now no condemnation to them which are in Christ Jesus, who walk not after the flesh, but after the Spirit. For the law of the Spirit of life in Christ Jesus hath made me free from the law of sin and death. For what the law could not do, in that it was weak through the flesh, God sending his own Son in the likeness of sinful flesh, and for sin, condemned sin in the flesh: That the righteousness of the law might be fulfilled in

---

[12] John Piper, "The Just Shall Live by Faith", October 31, 1982, *DesiringGod.org.*, accessed October 4, 2017, http://www.desiringgod.org/messages/the-just-shall-live-by-faith (Piper 1982)

us, who walk not after the flesh, but after the Spirit (Romans 8:1-4).

Therefore being justified by faith, we have peace with God through our Lord Jesus Christ: By whom also we have access by faith into this grace wherein we stand, and rejoice in hope of the glory of God (Romans 5:1-2).

"God declares sinners to be good in his sight if they have faith in Christ to save them from God's wrath. King David spoke of this, describing the happiness of an undeserving sinner who is declared "not guilty" by God. "Blessed and to be envied," he said, "are those whose sins are forgiven and put out of sight. Yes, what joy there is for anyone whose sins are no longer counted against him by the Lord." (Romans 4:5-8, TLB)

CONCLUDING THOUGHTS:

Let us as a nation, bow before God's mighty throne in repentance for our individual sins and the sins of our nation. Laying aside our selfish pride, seeking God's will for our lives and for our nation. Once more, let us take a stand for righteousness, teaching the gospel of Jesus Christ to our neighbors and our children; before it is too late.

Chapter 7:

When Does Trembling Fear Turn to Faith?

His questions answered, now Habakkuk stood before God. God's majesty, sovereignty, justice and righteousness shown forth in radiant Glory. There could be no more questions of why? No asking God for His reasoning. Now there was the reverent surrender to God's plan as it was laid out before Him, knowing of God's Grace throughout the ages that kept this planet suspended within the Universe. The very creator of all, reigned with power and majesty.

The magnitude of seeing God's Glory left Habakkuk with trembling fear. However, it filled his heart with overflowing hope, joy, and peace; because he also knew of God's Grace. True faith requires one to see God in magnificent glory with trembling fear at His Majestic Righteousness and Might. Then having seen His Glory, *as through a glass dimly* (2 Cor. 3:18), our hearts are overwhelmed with His Grace; turning our trembling fear to faith.

Grace could never be so sweet if we did not first stand before God with trembling fear because of our utter inability to look upon His Righteous Glorious Face without it.

When we consider the depth of depravity that lurks within man's soul. When we see the darkness of evil that surrounds our cities, our nation, and our world; should we not pause in trembling fear at its power? However, consider the truth: God has won the victory over sin, death, and evil's grip when Jesus Christ rose from the grave; having paid the penalty for sin and having lead *"captivity captives and (He) gave gifts to men"* (Ephesians 4:8). After considering this truth, our hearts must tremble at the Grace extended toward each of us; because, *"God so loved the world that He gave His Only Begotten Son, that whosoever believeth in him should not perish, but have everlasting life"* (John 3:16).

HABAKKUK'S TREMBLING FEAR THAT TURNED TO FAITH

In chapter three, Habakkuk's prayer is one of reverence, trembling fear before an Almighty, Righteous God who reigns with Justice, Holiness and Power. Habakkuk is fully aware now of God's plan of judgement upon His people for their continued sins. However, he is also aware that God has promised, "*the just shall live by his faith*" (Habakkuk 2:4).

It is in this knowledge, that Habakkuk begins his prayer, "*O LORD, I have heard thy speech, and was afraid: O LORD, revive thy work in the midst of the years, in the midst of the years make known; in wrath remember mercy*" (Habakkuk 3:2).

He recalls God's Power and Might, as He reigns over all things. Judgement would come upon the people of Judah. That was certain at this point. However, Habakkuk knew that Grace would reign for all who believe, whose faith would give them life. That was when Habakkuk could say,

Effie Darlene Barba

HABAKKUK 3: 16-19

> *When I heard, my belly trembled; my lips quivered at the voice: rottenness entered into my bones, and I trembled in myself, that I might rest in the day of trouble: when he cometh up unto the people, he will invade them with his troops.*
>
> *Although the fig tree shall not blossom, neither shall fruit be in the vines; the labour of the olive shall fail, and the fields shall yield no meat; the flock shall be cut off from the fold, and there shall be no herd in the stalls:*
>
> *Yet I will rejoice in the LORD, I will joy in the God of my salvation. The LORD God is my strength, and he will make my feet like hinds' feet, and he will make me to walk upon mine high places.*

TODAY'S EVIL AND GOD'S RESPONSE

When we consider all the evil that surrounds us, from the shooter in Las Vegas, the North Korean Dictator, and the Isis terrorists. Yes, we have seen the face of pure evil. Also, we have seen natural disasters. Habakkuk knew, the righteous faith-filled people of God were about to face captivity; along with all those who had sought after self-pleasures, denying the righteous, power of Almighty God. However, his hope and joy held tight to the promises of God.

> *"For the vision is yet for an appointed time, but at the end it shall speak, and not lie: though it tarry, wait for it: because it will surely come... For the earth shall be filled with the knowledge of the Glory of the Lord"* (Habakkuk 2:3,14).

God will return one day. On this truth, the people of God can stand with hope, joy and faith. For those who do not know Jesus Christ as Lord and Savior, this is a wakeup call. Pure evil forces one to awaken to the false narratives of relativism. There cannot be pure evil, if there are no moral standards by which to judge. Pure evil contrasts against a Righteous, Holy God.

HABAKKUK'S TREMBLING FEAR POINTED TOWARD FAITH IN CHRIST

John Piper points out in his sermon, *The Just Shall Live by Faith:*

> Habakkuk couldn't see ahead to how God would preserve both his holy hatred for sin and his merciful forgiveness of sinners who trust him. But God had revealed it, and so he proclaimed it: the just shall gain their lives in the judgment by faith. He knew that when he called them "just," they weren't sinless. He

meant that those who are right with God in spite of their sin are those who trust God for his mercy. But how can a holy God, who hates sin, show eternal mercy on sinners who simply trust him for mercy? God did not reveal that much to Habakkuk.

The New Testament Revelation of the Gospel

But he did to the apostle Paul, and the answer is the death of Christ. Paul said it like this:

They are justified by his grace as a gift, through the redemption which is in Christ Jesus, whom God put forward as an expiation by his blood, to be received by faith. This was to show God's righteousness, because in his divine forbearance he had passed over former sins; it was to prove at the present time that he himself is righteous and that he justifies him who has faith in Jesus" (Romans 3:24-26) Let me try to translate that into your situation. When you put your trust in Jesus Christ as your Savior and Lord, when you give up trying to lead your own life and establish your own worth, and instead surrender your heart to him and bank on him for your future, three things happen. 1) Your sin receives its deserved condemnation. 2) God's righteousness receives its deserved glorification. 3) And you receive your undeserved justification.[13]

CONCLUSION

All God's people can stand firm with hope, joy, and peace; no matter how dark the road may seem. For those who do not know Jesus Christ as Savior; today is the day of

---

[13] John Piper, *The Just Shall Live by Faith*

salvation, if only you will ask Him in. Let your trembling fear be turned to faith, hope and joy.

Jesus said, "*Behold, I stand at the door, and knock: if any man hear my voice, and open the door, I will come in to him, and will sup with him, and he with me*" Revelation 3:20

Effie Darlene Barba

Chapter 8:

God's Glory Revealed in Justice and Mercy

Whenever we attempt to compartmentalize God's Glory by placing one aspect higher than another; we risk losing the truth of God. All too often, when viewing the diverse excellencies of God's justice in contrast with His mercy; Christians see this as a hard to rationalize dichotomy. Particularly, in our modern society and church; there is a social drive toward only speaking of God's love and never His wrath against sin. The dichotomy between God's Mercy and Justice is not itself a false theology; because, God's Glory shines radiantly from His just and righteous nature, as much as from His merciful grace toward sinful man. However, a false theology develops when either His Mercy or His Justice is espoused as denying the other.

Yet, here in modern Western culture, we see too many churches falling head first into the theological trap of presenting God's Love and mercy to the exclusion of His justice. It is as if His justice is something to be left unspoken of for fear that people will not come. Many Christians speak of God's mercy and love; while ignoring His righteousness, justice and hatred toward sin.

When the church focuses only on God's loving mercy to the exclusion of His justice; it risks falling headlong into a counterfeit theology, where the true God becomes unrecognizable. Balancing and viewing God's justice and mercy as equally beautiful aspects of His Glory, is paramount to living a life reflecting His Glory and is key to the Church presenting the gospel of Christ to a world in need of a Savior.

God cannot be loving, if He is not also just.

UNDERSTANDING GRACE THROUGH THE EYES OF JUSTICE

How can anyone truly know or feel the depth of God's Grace and Mercy toward them, if they do not know of His wrath against sin? If only His Mercy is presented; how, can anyone realize their need of a Savior? God knows that ultimate delight in Him can never be complete until one can see His Glory fully displayed in both His Justice and His Grace toward them: (sinners, incapable of even fulfilling the first commandment, to love God with all their heart, their soul and to put no other God before Him). (Exodus 20:3, Deuteronomy 6:4-6)

When we forget or diminish His Justice, while focusing on only His love and mercy; we allow false theology to be born. Some such doctrines seen in our modern-day churches include the prosperity gospel, the tolerance doctrines, and relativism. In a *"A Little Book for New*

Theologians", Kelly Kapic warns us of just such error as he describes God's response to Israel relative to their worship depicted in Isaiah 1. Mr. Kapic wrote, "They have misunderstood Yahweh by not mirroring His heart, thus turning all their actions and words into corrupted religion."[14] So, the question again arises, "Can we begin to know God's heart, if we don't first bow reverently before His Throne of Justice?"

THE RISK OF FORGETTING JUSTICE

Focusing only upon God's Mercy, Love and Grace; the modern day church risks the influx of a relativism that diminishes the devastation that sin effects in the heart of mankind; thus, disavowing the magnificent beauty of the

---

[14] ¹Kelly M. Kapic, *A Little Book for New Theologians* (Downers Grove, IL: IVP Academic, 2012), 87. (Kapic 2012)

Cross. Beyond that, it opens the floodgates for Atheistic critics who say, "a loving God could not allow this or that". Furthermore, focusing only on God's loving mercy leads one to believe somehow, they deserve His love. Then, pride overtakes the sweet humility that comes from seeing God's just wrath against sin; while, at the same time paying the price of salvation to all who would come. Or the sweet joy of discovering that God graciously had loved and made a way for sinners.

"Our study of the Bible is meant to build our relationship to God"[15] "Part of the theologian's task is to make sure our faith does not confuse cultural contingencies with normative continuities."[16]

---

[15] Kapic, New Theologians, 113
[16] Ibid.,95

WHAT IF WE FOCUS ON JUSTICE ALONE?

Neither can we become so focused on His wrath and judgment that we forsake His Unmerited Grace toward all, bidding them to come. God hates sin; because, it separates the creature from knowing Him. Therefore, His hatred of sin reflects His love; because, He desires our fullest happiness. And, God knows; there is no true joy apart from Him. *"Not unto us, O Lord, not unto us, but unto thy name give glory, for thy mercy, and for thy truth's sake. Wherefore should the heathen say, 'Where is now their God?' But our God is in the heavens: he hath done whatsoever he hath pleased"* (Psalm 115:1-3). All that God allows, He does so that mankind might see a glimpse of His Glory and desire it. He knows that nothing else can satisfy the longing of our souls, apart from Him.

GOD'S GLORY REVEALED

"It is a proper and excellent thing for infinite glory to shine forth; and for the same reason, it is proper that the shining forth of God's glory should be complete; that is, that all parts of his glory should shine forth, that every beauty should be proportionably effulgent [=radiant], that the beholder may have a proper notion of God. It is not proper that one glory should be exceedingly manifested, and another not at all"[17] --Jonathan Edwards

To reconcile this dichotomy, Kelly Kapic suggests, "we must never forget that the purpose of the words are to draw us to the word and thus into the embrace of the triune

---

[17] Jonathan Edwards, "Concerning the Divine Decrees", *The Works of Jonathan Edwards* (Edinburgh, Scotland: Banner of Truth, 1974), p. 528 (Edwards 1974)

God....that we might know the true God and respond to Him in repentance and faith."[18]

DO YOU KNOW HIM?

Do you know God as your heavenly Father? Do you know the sweetness of sitting in His presence? God is the joy and love our hearts so desire; if only, we would seek Him above all else.

Consider this: Adam and Eve walked in the garden daily with God, saw Him; yet, did not fully understand the magnitude of His Glory. Because they never knew anything else. Can you truly appreciate light had you never seen darkness? Just as darkness is the absence of light, evil is the absence of God. Our world has not yet consumed itself in pure evil; because of God's love, mercy and light shining into

---

[18] Kapic, New Theologians,117

the darkness of this world. Every act of kindness, every piece of beauty is evidence of God's hand of mercy and grace still standing in suspension holding us in place—His covenant to mankind.

We cry out to God from the dark night, seeking Mercy. However, He remains upon His throne. Why is it that when all is well, we forget He is the only truth and light; without Him, there is no hope of light! Come, let us seek Him while it is still day; that, He may be the hope, the joy, and the light that guides our path. I wrote this poem, from a saddened heart. All around us we see evil, anger and sorrow. If only we would turn and run to our Savior, He has promised, *"Then shall ye call upon me, and ye shall go and pray unto me, and I will hearken unto you. And ye shall seek me, and find me, when ye shall search for me with all your heart* (Jeremiah 29:12-13).

From the Dark of the Night, for Mercy We Cry

by Effie Darlene Barba

From the Dark of the Night, for Your Mercy We Cry

As we look to the heavens and scream out, "Lord, Why?"

Why so much evil, such suffering and pain

Won't You reach down in Might, to this evil restrain

Before our dear nation doth fall like the rest

When we once had been known, as Christians, the best

Then God Replied,

"Look there around you, Oh, do you not see?

That You all have forgotten to focus on me

So, busy you run from life to and fro

While seeking great treasures and idols below

Have You forgotten I am truth and light?

Without me, there is only darkness of night!

When you shut out my presence all you will see

Is evil remaining: the absence of me!

How is it then, that you would forget?

I AM all you need for peace, love and joy; yet

You only seek me when your life is beset

By sorrows so filled with pain and regret

Effie Darlene Barba

Did I not give you my all, that you might be set free?

From the evil and pain that you find without me

You struggle through trials, so filled with strife

While I stand here to offer you a new life

From the nothingness, darkness in all that you see

True being can only be found in me

I sent you my Son who died on a cross

To pay for your sins, at such a high cost

Because of my love, I gave you my best

That then within me you your heart could find rest

There can never be Grace without Justice, you see

For evil does reign in the absence of me

I cannot deny my righteousness, child

For evil would then unchained run a wild

It is an act of my grace, the earth does still spin

Awaiting one more heart for to win

Turn from your sins and seek me, my face

There you will find perfect love, joy and grace

CONCLUDING THOUGHTS:

In the absence of righteousness, pure evil exists. That being true, why do we not seek God who is Righteousness. Without Him, nothingness exists; blackness of the heart and soul. Although, we may pretend or present ourselves as otherwise; because, His Grace has extended itself to reach out and demonstrate His Glory through men and women. At times, those who have not believed, are given by Grace a glimpse of true love in their own hearts; but that is a gift of grace by a loving God. However, if God removed His hand of Grace for a second in time; this world would plunge into utter darkness, chaos as evil took over. So, we must turn from the dark night to seek His face!

ISAIAH 29:15,19,23-24

> *Woe unto them that seek deep to hide their counsel from the Lord, and their works are in the dark, and they say, Who seeth us? and who knoweth us? The meek also shall increase their joy in the Lord, and the poor among men shall rejoice in the Holy One of Israel. But when he seeth his children, the work of mine hands, in the midst of him, they shall sanctify my name, and sanctify the Holy One of Jacob, and shall fear the God of Israel. They also that erred in spirit shall come*

to understanding, and they that murmured shall learn doctrine.

ISAIAH 30:12-15,18-21

Wherefore thus saith the Holy One of Israel, Because ye despise this word, and trust in oppression and perverseness, and stay thereon: Therefore this iniquity shall be to you as a breach ready to fall, swelling out in a high wall, whose breaking cometh suddenly at an instant. And he shall break it as the breaking of the potters' vessel that is broken in pieces; he shall not spare: so that there shall not be found in the bursting of it a sherd to take fire from the hearth, or to take water withal out of the pit.

[15] **For thus saith the Lord God, the Holy One of Israel; In returning and rest shall ye be**

saved; in quietness and in confidence shall be your strength: and ye would not.

[18] And therefore will the Lord wait, that he may be gracious unto you, and therefore will he be exalted, that he may have mercy upon you: for the Lord is a God of judgment: blessed are all they that wait for him.

For the people shall dwell in Zion at Jerusalem: thou shalt weep no more: he will be very gracious unto thee at the voice of thy cry; when he shall hear it, he will answer thee.

[20] And though the Lord give you the bread of adversity, and the water of affliction, yet shall not thy teachers be removed into a corner any more, but thine eyes shall see thy teachers:

²¹And thine ears shall hear a word behind thee, saying, This is the way, walk ye in it, when ye turn to the right hand, and when ye turn to the left.

Effie Darlene Barba

Chapter 9:

When Justice Must Reign for Love to Be Complete

Love can never be truly fulfilled unless justice stands true. God must remain true to His righteous nature; therein, justice and truth must reign. In the days of Jonah, God reached out to a cruel, unrighteous Nineveh with love. Nineveh was a gentile city, the capital of the Assyrian Empire. It was located very near the modern-day Mosul.

God sent Jonah to foretell of their coming doom unless they repented of their sins. Miraculously, they turned to God in repentance and the entire city was saved; because, of the revival that followed Jonah's preaching. That was somewhere between 100 to 150 years before the book of Nahum. However, the revival was short lived; just as it was in Judea during the reign of Josiah. Now, this gentile city once more faced judgement, as would Judah. Love could never be perfected unless justice and righteousness reigned.

God had saved the city of Nineveh; however, the light of truth only shown for a brief period and now Nahum predicts their demise. God did not send Nahum to the city as He had Jonah. Why? J. Vernon McGee remarks as to the difference:

> He (God) sent Jonah to Ninevah because Nineveh was a great wicked city, but they were totally ignorant of God. When the message was brought, the city turned to God, all the way from the king on the throne to the peasant in the hovel. As a result, God spared the city. Now 100 to 150 years have gone by, and the city has relapsed and returned back to its old way. Why doesn't Nahum go? Because they have already had the light, and they've rejected it.[19]

---

[19] McGee, *Thru the Bible,* 813

FROM LIGHT TO UTTER DARKNESS

Jesus said, *"The light of the body is the eye: if therefore thine eye be single, thy whole body shall be full of light. But if thine eye be evil, thy whole body shall be full of darkness. If therefore the light that is in thee be darkness, how great is that darkness!"* (Matthew 6:23).

Once we have seen the light of truth presented and turn from it; the darkness intensifies. Once we have heard the gospel and rejected it; darkness intensifies as it is chosen over light. Evil grows and intensifies when we reject the truth. A loving God sent forth the light; however, once His love is rejected and cast aside, the only thing that remains is judgement.

No nation has been so blessed by God's light of truth than ours. The United States of America was founded on Godly principles. America's Christian principles led to our abolishing slavery and oppression. Beyond that, as a nation we grew in power, prosperity, and generosity. However, somewhere along the way; we forgot the very principles on which we began. Alas, where do we stand now.

THE RISE AND FALL OF A NATION

No nation can stand; unless, they remain faithful to those principles set out by God. Alexander Fraser Tytler was a Scottish born lawyer and writer who is quoted as saying,

> A democracy cannot exist as a permanent form of government. It can only exist until the voters discover that they can vote themselves largesse from the public treasury. From that moment on, the majority always votes for the candidates promising the most benefits from the public treasury with the result that a democracy always collapses over loose fiscal policy, always followed by a dictatorship. The average age of the world's greatest civilizations has been 200 years. These nations have progressed through this sequence: From

bondage to spiritual faith; From spiritual faith to great courage; From courage to liberty; From liberty to abundance; From abundance to selfishness; From selfishness to apathy; From apathy to dependence; From dependence back into bondage.[20]

Where are we as a nation along this pendulum? Have we not moved from abundance to selfishness? Or have we allowed apathy to begin? We, the Christians have stood by quietly, allowing the schools to teach and encourage Socialism which will lead once more to bondage. Have we forgotten all that we once stood for? In the name of freedom, we allow our voices to be silenced by the far left! We have forgotten that for love to be perfected, we must stand firm for justice and righteousness. We stand by idly by while the left wants

---

[20] Alexander Fraser Tytler, "Alexander Fraser Tytler: Quotable Quotes," *Goodread.com,* accessed October 9, 2017, https://www.goodreads.com/quotes/108530-a-democracy-cannot-exist-as-a-permanent-form-of-government (Tytler n.d.)

to destroy the history of having moved from spiritual faith, leading to courage and the fight for liberty. Unfortunately, the Democratic Party has moved so far left; because, their desire for power wishes to place all of us in the bondage of big government, dependent on them for everything. Ruled by their ideologies.

FROM LIBERTY TO BONDAGE:

When Justice is ignored, there is no true Love

So, many unknowing people cry out that we must allow illegal immigration to continue that we might continue to have "cheap labor" to do the jobs we find too menial. Many would prefer welfare than to do labor; however, do we not see the truth? By thus doing, we enslave a people, we encourage the "coyote trade" which robs and steals from the most vulnerable, we forget the children who die in the desert, or the families that live ten to a room.

Even as a small child I remember a migrant worker with five hungry children clinging to him who could not cash the check given him by the farmer; because, the farmer had cheated him. I cried loudly protesting to my mother, asking "Why?" She replied, "Some people are evil and the farmer who did this is one of them."

How can we call it love; if, we deny that which is just and right? If there are no laws to abide by; then, there are no laws to protect. We cannot justify a new form of slavery and abuse; because, we are too selfish to see the truth.

I lived many years in Mexico and dearly love the people. When I moved to Mexico, I registered my children there; because, their Father was a Mexican Citizen (although permanent resident of the USA). To send the parents back, does not require separation of families. They merely need to register their children in Mexico; using their citizenship and the child's Birth Certificate. To not uphold and stand for laws and demand only legal immigration, is to endorse a new form of slavery and oppression of a people.

CONCLUSION:

As we look at the book of Nahum, we must consider how this is true of our nation as well. Where are we on the pendulum? Having had the great light of the truth of the gospel with so many churches to shine that light; have we now begun to allow darkness to overcome that light. Will we heed the warnings: take a stand, saluting our flag as we proclaim our pledge of allegiance?

""I pledge allegiance to the Flag of the United States of America, and to the Republic for which it stands, one Nation under God, indivisible, with **liberty and justice for all**."

Chapter 10:

How Can Words of Comfort Really Be an Admonition?

Nineveh, a major gentile city in Assyria found God through the preaching of Jonah. How long did revival last? One generation had found God; yet, they failed somehow to teach that knowledge to the next generation. The great revival had occurred somewhere between 772 and 754 B.C. Yet, by 697 B.C., they were known as a cruel, bloody nation.

Meanwhile in the land of Judah; Manasseh had become King. King Manasseh of Judah returned the people to idolatry. Because of the nation turning their back on God, they were overtaken by the cruel Assyrians. Two nations stood in the crux of judgement because of their choice.

How can one then find comfort in the words of Nahum? His name meant comforter and his words were meant to comfort the remnant of true believers that remained in Judah. Yet, they come with an admonition for us to teach our children well.

We can read in 2 Kings 21 of the corruption of Manasseh, from idolatry to the shedding of innocent blood. A tyrannical King whom many of the people of Judah followed with great fervor. Evil filled the streets and God proclaimed:

2 Kings 21: 10-12

> *And the LORD spake by his servants the prophets, saying,*
>
> *Because Manasseh king of Judah hath done these abominations, and hath done wickedly above all that the Amorites did, which were before him, and hath made Judah also to sin with his idols: Therefore, thus saith the LORD God of Israel, Behold, I am bringing such evil upon Jerusalem and Judah,*

that whosoever heareth of it, both his ears shall tingle.

Manasseh was later carried away in chains and subsequently repented of his sins. He tried to restore worship; however, his own son followed in the ways of evil. Rather than to have learned from his father's errors, he continued in evil.

During that same era in history, Assyria rose in their evil endeavors to become the cruelest nation in the area. They wreaked havoc throughout the land of Judah.

TWO NATIONS UNDER GOD,

TURNED FROM GOD TO SEEK EVIL

The revival in Nineveh was short-lived. In 722, King Sennacherib besieged Samaria and defeated it, overtaking the Northern Kingdom of Israel. Then "21 years later (in 701) Sennacherib (705-681) invaded Judah and destroyed 46 Judean towns and cities. After encircling Jerusalem, 185,000 of Sennacherib's soldiers were killed overnight and Sennacherib returned to Nineveh."[21] Nineveh underwent a moment of grace; however, 150 years later "Nineveh was the capital of one of the cruelest, vilest, most powerful, and most idolatrous empires in the world."[21] They were known for skinning people alive, cutting off heads, and even burying people in the desert with only their head above sand and their tongue staked to the ground before them.

NAHUM'S WORDS OF COMFORT

The entire book of Nahum prophecies the destruction of Nineveh: God's words of comfort to the remnant of people who trusted and followed Him. Soon, a child would become King of Judah for a time. His name Josiah. Although his father did evil, and he was the grandson of Manasseh; who had led the nation into the worst forms of

---

[21] Alexander Fraser Tytler, "Alexander Fraser Tytler: Quotable Quotes," *Goodread.com,* accessed October 9,2017, https://www.goodreads.com/quotes/108530-a-democracy-cannot-exist-as-a-permanent-form-of-government (Johnson 2004)

idolatry; King Josiah would lead a generation of His people into a great revival. During that revival period, Nineveh would fall; just as Nahum spoke of.

The future of our nation, depends on you and I teaching the younger generation to love God, above all else. We see what happened to two nations who once were given the light of God's Grace; when they failed to teach the truth to the generations that followed. How can we stand by idly while our schools and Universities teach relativism? How can we not teach our Children of God's Grace and His Justice? To teach God's truth, we must first study, pray and grow in His word ourselves. We must not be afraid, and we must boldly stand for Christ, in a land that some desire to silence our voices.

[1] Elliot Johnson, "Nahum", *The Bible Knowledge Commentary: An Exposition of the Scriptures by Dallas Seminary Faculty: Old Testament,* John Walvoord and Roy Zuck, eds., (Colorado Springs: CO: Victor, 2004), 1493

[2] Ibid., 1494.

Effie Darlene Barba

Chapter 11:

How to Know a Revival of Faith When All Seems Lost?

The Covenant Love and Mercy of God stands firm to those who are His people. Judah had turned their backs on God during the reigns of Manasseh and Amon. Instead they chose to worship idols. This had been the story of God's people throughout the Old Testament. God would rescue and save His people; extending His mighty hand of mercy repeatedly.

During the reigns of Manasseh and Amon, the Assyrians with great cruelty attacked with brutality and force against the people of Judah. There appeared to be no hope, as evil seemed to be winning against them. Nahum foretold of the fall of Nineveh and the Assyrian nation. God would step in to save His people; because of His Mercy and His Covenantal Love for them. Right before His judgement against Nineveh was enacted in 612, a young King Josiah would lead the nation in revival.

What battles are you facing today? Do the mountains before you seem impassable? Joni Eareckson Tada has lived a lifetime in a wheelchair since her accident left her a quadriplegic at the age of 18. She has battled with chronic pain, disability; and even, breast cancer. One might wonder how a loving God could allow such tragedy and suffering in one of His children. Yet, her ministry stands as a portrait of Grace as she presses on. Her smile and her courage shine forth with His Radiant Glory being shown to the world. She speaks with great power as she tells the world that her suffering transforms her heart, sifting away the chaff and burning it. Her pain has driven her to the cross where she has found great joy amid her pain and suffering. Recently she published a Study Bible titled, *Beyond Suffering Bible*.

In her comments introducing the book of Nahum, Joni Eareckson Tada wrote:

> God is faithful to his people, even though they constantly wander away from their covenant

relationship. No matter how many times they stray from the truth, God is relentless in his efforts to bring his people back into his fold. This should provide great comfort for those who believe that their circumstances set them outside of God's reach. Nothing could be further from the truth.[22]

God knows that our heart cannot be satisfied until we find our being and life in Him. He is willing to allow whatever it takes to awaken His people from their slumber. We look around us to see such evil present in the world, from ISIS to North Korea. Trembling at the thought of Iran and North Korea gaining nuclear power; we would stand hopeless were it not for our knowing the truth: God Wins. In fact, He already has, and we know the end of the story.

---

[22] Joni Eareckson Tada, "Features and Bible Helps", *Beyond Suffering Bible,* (Carol Streams, IL: Tyndale House, 2016), 1050 (Tada 2016)

Just as Nahum accurately foretold of the fall of Nineveh long before it happened; we know that one-day Christ will return and take His people to be with Him. He will establish His Kingdom on earth and one-day all our tears will be turned to Joy, living in His Glorious Presence. Beyond that, He promises all who put their faith in Him can live with peace, joy and hope on this earth. This should make us fearless to stand upon the foundation of His Covenantal Love and Grace toward us.

GOD'S ANGER AND REVENGE AGAINST EVIL

"The burden of Nineveh. The book of the vision of Nahum the Elkoshite. God is jealous, and the LORD revengeth; the LORD revengeth, and is furious; the LORD will take vengeance on his adversaries, and he reserveth wrath for his enemies.

The LORD is slow to anger, and great in power, and will not at all acquit the wicked: the LORD hath his way in the whirlwind and in the storm, and the clouds are the dust of his feet" (Nahum 1:1-3).

Even when it looks as though evil may win, it will not. Because of God's Mercy reaching out to the lost, we sometimes think He has turned away. However, we must remember in His Mercy, He calls sinners to repent. He did just that when He sent Jonah to Nineveh.

For a brief time, they turned to God. How many people were saved? How many eternities transformed? Yet, the city quickly turned away from God. After such a great revival and having seen the light; how dark now, was their darkness. It is that way when mankind, having seen the light seeks darkness.

GOD REIGNS OVER THE LAND AND THE SEA

> *"He rebuketh the sea, and maketh it dry, and drieth up all the rivers: Bashan languisheth, and Carmel, and the flower of Lebanon languisheth. The mountains quake at him, and the hills melt, and the earth is burned at his presence, yea, the world, and all that dwell therein.*
>
> *Who can stand before his indignation? and who can abide in the fierceness of his anger? his fury is poured out like fire, and the rocks are thrown down by him"* (Nahum 1:4-6).

We see the devastation from hurricanes, wild fires and earthquakes upon our land and the world. The face of pure evil has been seen in the Las Vegas shootings, the violence in Chicago, Isis terrorism around the globe, and in the cruelty of Kim Jong-Un against not only his people, but those he has held prisoner. Despite all that, we can trust in God. No evil can stand before His indignation and anger. When His steadying hand of grace lets go; all evil will be destroyed, for judgement will come.

God spoke in Deuteronomy 32:35, "*To me belongeth vengeance and recompence; their foot shall slide in due time: for the day of their calamity is at hand, and the things that shall come upon them make haste.*"

In due time, their foot shall slide. We can cling tight to that promise, trusting in the Sovereign God who spoke this. He tarries in His enactment of judgement; because, of Grace, awaiting one more sinner to repent. That Grace is the same He extended toward us; drawing us to His side. We should never be discontent or impatient with His Heart of Mercy. What price is too great for us to pay or suffering too great for the salvation of one soul?

A STRONGHOLD FOR HIS BELOVED: A STRONG TOWER FROM THE ENEMY

The LORD is good, a strong hold in the day of trouble; and he knoweth them that trust in him (Nahum 1:7).

Could there be any more comforting words than that? "*The name of the LORD is a strong tower: the righteous runneth into it, and is safe*" (Proverbs 18:10).

Hear my cry, O God; attend unto my prayer. From the end of the earth will I cry unto thee, when my heart is overwhelmed: lead me to the rock that is higher than I. For thou hast been a shelter for me, and a strong tower from the enemy. I will abide in thy tabernacle for ever: I will trust in the covert of thy wings. Selah (Psalm 61:1-4).

Lead me to the rock when my heart is overwhelmed; because, He is my strong tower. Are you overwhelmed today? Trust in the covert of His wings. He covers you with His righteousness, protects you from the enemy, and promises you His best; if only, you turn to Him. Do you know Him?

Effie Darlene Barba

Chapter 12:

How to Bring a Revival of Hope When All Seems Lost?

Israel had been overtaken by the Assyrians and now Judah lay in ruble. The nation had turned their eyes away from God, seeking other pleasures and worshipping idols of gold. All would appear to be lost; when Nahum comes with his message of destruction to Nineveh and a hope for revival in Jerusalem and all of Judea.

Wherein lay that hope? What message brought the people to their knees in prayer; ultimately, with God bringing revival through King Josiah? It was this: *"Behold upon the mountains the feet of him that bringeth good tidings, that publisheth peace! O Judah, keep thy solemn feasts, perform thy vows: for the wicked shall no more pass through thee; he is utterly cut off"* (Nahum 1:15). The messiah will come as promised. It may look as though all is lost; but, God is not done, and He has the final victory.

We look around us at all the evil and corruption inside our dear country and the world. Disheartened by it all, we too cry out. There seems to be no answer at times. We wonder where God is amid all this pain and sorrow. Yet, He is there bidding His messengers to go forth and proclaim the good news of Jesus Christ to our nation and to the world.

Christ came, just as promised! He died, paying once and for all the penalty of our sins! Arising from the grave, victorious over sin and death; He sits on His throne at the right hand of His Father, making intercession for us (Romans 8:34). We are being called forth to be a Nahum spreading the good news of the gospel message. Christ is returning to establish His reign. Peace will come!

ASSURANCE: GOD NEVER CHANGES!

The promises of God stood true yesterday and they will be done, as He has promised.

Nineveh and the Assyrian army fell in 612 B.C. Every detail of their destruction from the floods to the fires occurred exactly as predicted. On page 1495 of *The Bible Knowledge Commentary*, there is laid out a diagram of the verses and their historical fulfillment.[23] As exact as God fulfilled His vision to Nahum, He also fulfilled His promises that Babylon would fall as outlined by both Isaiah and Jeremiah (Isaiah 13, Jeremiah 50-51). Furthermore, long before Cyrus was born; God had spoken his name as the one gentile king who would free the children of Israel from bondage and provide for them what would be needed to rebuild. (Isaiah 44:28, Ezra 1:1).

Note this. This is the same God who promises us that one-day Christ will return. In fact, He uses some of the same words. In Nahum 1:15, he spoke of the messiah. "Nahum says this in reference to Assyria and you will find that Isaiah actually uses the same expression"[24]

---

[23] Johnson, "Nahum", 1495
[24] McGee, *Thru the Bible*, 823

> *"How beautiful upon the mountains are the feet of him that bringeth good tidings, that publisheth peace; that bringeth good tidings of good, that publisheth salvation; that saith unto Zion, Thy God reigneth!* (Isaiah 52:7).

J. Vernon McGee writes:

> "I think Nahum was the first to say this and then Isaiah. Finally, Paul quotes Isaiah and makes a different application of it in the section of his epistle that refers to Israel, that is in the dispensational section of Romans. Paul is arguing there that God is not through with the nation Israel and that in the future there will again come to them the good tidings of great joy. But it is also a worldwide message applicable to today.[25]

---

[25] McGee, *Thru the Bible*, 823

A MESSAGE OF REVIVAL FOR NOW!

Paul referring to these verses in Nahum and Isaiah takes it one step further and commissions each of us to be the feet bringing good tidings. We are to be the feet who climb whatever mountains that lie before us to spread the truth of the gospel message to the world and to proclaim the victory. Christ will return, alleluia; but, until that day, we must speak forth His truth and bring revival to our faith and all people. Look at what Paul wrote:

> *For there is no difference between the Jew and the Greek: for the same Lord over all is rich unto all that call upon him. For whosoever shall call upon the name of the Lord shall be saved. How then shall they call on him in whom they have not believed? and how shall they believe in him of whom they have not heard? and how shall they hear without a preacher? And how shall they*

preach, except they be sent? as it is written, How beautiful are the feet of them that preach the gospel of peace, and bring glad tidings of good things! (Romans 10:12-15).

HOW WILL REVIVAL COME?

1. We the people who know Christ Jesus as Lord and Savior, must be on our knees praying for our nation! *"If my people, which are called by my name, shall humble themselves, and pray, and seek my face, and turn from their wicked ways; then will I hear from heaven, and will forgive their sin, and will heal their land"* (2 Chronicles 7:14). We must in humility, seek forgiveness for our own sins and those of our nation.

2. We must study God's Word. *"Study to shew thyself approved unto God, a workman that needeth not to be ashamed, rightly dividing the word of truth"* (2 Timothy 2:15).

3. We must Go, climb whatever mountains lie before us and then shout the good news of the gospel for all to hear. Until Christ returns, we have been called to be the messengers of hope in the world. Revival cannot come, unless we boldly proclaim the name of Christ in our nation and the world. *"Go ye into all the world, and preach the gospel to every creature"* (Mark 16:15).

Effie Darlene Barba

Chapter 13:

When Evil Begins Within, The Walls Are Broken. How?

Nineveh that great city who experienced a revival during the days of Jonah, now faced the full wrath of God. Nahum foretells of their destruction with detail in chapter 2 of his vision. Chapter 1 gives us a clue of how this all began within; while chapter 2 details the fall of that city. Although, God had for a moment withheld his hand of grace toward Israel and Judah; He has now returned in wrath against Nineveh for all their evil deeds in their attempt to destroy God's people.

Following their great revival, this gentile nation now would see their walls broken down because of allowing evil to overtake their hearts while forgetting the very God who presented to them grace 150 years prior. Now evil reigns within and their terror is spread throughout the neighboring lands.

Evil begins with such subtlety. From within arises ideologies that first sound good; but, lead to full destruction of any semblance of faith in the very God who presented His grace and light of hope. God spoke of this through Nahum when he wrote:

> *There is one come out of thee, that imagineth evil against the Lord, a wicked counsellor. Thus, saith the Lord; Though they be quiet, and likewise many, yet thus shall they be cut down, when he shall pass through. Though I have afflicted thee, I will afflict thee no more. For now will I break his yoke from off thee, and will burst thy bonds in sunder* (Nahum 1:11-13).

The yoke against Israel would be broken and Assyria would be destroyed; because, God's people would return to worship Him under the leadership of King Josiah.

THE PARALLEL BETWEEN NINEVEH AND JUDAH

Evil enters quietly through wicked counsellors. It had within the nation of Israel; where, in times of prosperity the people allowed their hearts to be drawn aside. The truth is distorted, and people's hearts are turned against the God of grace who has provided for them, shepherded them, and upheld them. Thus, God justly withheld His hand of grace as described in Nahum 2:2. Blinded by their own evil hearts, the nation of Israel stood on the brink of utter destruction.

What about Nineveh? Was it not the same? God had shown forth His light and revival had swept the city; however, they turned from light to the utter darkness of evil. No longer was there even a shimmer of light left.

The people of God would return to worship Him for a time, under the wise counsel of King Josiah. Thus, Judah was saved, and Nineveh destroyed by God; because, Nineveh loved darkness rather than light.

> *And this is the condemnation, that light is come into the world, and men loved darkness rather than light, because their deeds were evil. For every one that doeth evil hateth the light, neither cometh to the light, lest his deeds should be reproved* (John 3:19-20).

WHAT ABOUT THE USA

So, what about the United States of America. Have we not through subtle, quiet counselors begun to lay aside our faith in God. There are those who would in the name of peace and love; protest all of God's commands. Our nation born on Christian principles; now questioned or assigned ulterior motives. Indeed, our Declaration of Independence and Constitution formed a foundation of faith in God first. All that we fought and ultimately abolished: slavery, tyranny, and governmental reign over men's faith; because of God's people rising to shine light into darkness and overcome evil with God's goodness.

Now we have many who want to erase that history. They wish to insinuate that we are at the core an evil society. Some would say all the years standing as a beacon of light to the world, all the generosity, the missionary work, and our stance for life only demonstrated evil ideologies. Furthermore, they want to erase God from all the history books. Where will we stand when darkness has overcome the light?

WHEN EVIL GREW WITHIN, THE WALLS BROKEN

As we look at God's judgement on Nineveh, we cannot help but see some parallels between them and us. First, as he describes their destruction in Nahum 2: 4

> *The chariots shall rage in the streets, they shall justle one against another in the broad ways: they shall seem like torches, they shall run like the lightnings* (Nahum 2:4).

The destruction of Nineveh began with rioting in the streets. People in their chariots wreaking havoc upon their city. There was drunkenness and lascivious living. *"For while they be folden together as thorns, and while they are drunken as drunkards, they shall be devoured as stubble fully dry* (Nahum 1:10).

Furthermore, the rioting within left the walls unprotected. The walls were broken down; then, their enemies could enter in and destroy them.

Robert Calkins wrote, "Nahum portrays (the) siege, reproduces its horrors and its savagery, its cruelties and mercilessness, in language so realistic that one is able to see it and feel it. First comes the fighting in the suburbs. Then the assault upon the walls. (Followed by) the capture of the city and its destruction."[26]

Shouldn't that awaken your heart to seek God? Two nations stood. One heeded the warning and turned to God; while, the other did not. Destruction followed; because, justice would reign. First began the rioting in the streets; then, the walls fell. Once the walls break, destruction follows.

---

[26] Robert Calkins, *The Modern Message of the Minor Prophets,* (New York: Harper & Brothers, 1947), 82 (Calkins 1947)

Effie Darlene Barba

Chapter 14:

An Evil Nation Destroyed by Just Righteousness Why?

The case for God's Righteousness and Justice in judging nations is clearly presented in chapter 3 of Nahum. He had shown such mercy and grace to Nineveh when he sent Jonah to preach many years before. They had seen the love and light of God shine upon them with great sweeping salvation. Still, the subsequent generations turned from light to darkness; seeking power and riches.

Instead of the succeeding generations following God, they grew in pride and selfishness. They became a brutal city, filled with lies, bloodshed, tyranny and violence. John Steinbeck in *The Winter of Our Discontent* wrote, "It's so much darker when a light goes out than it would have been if it had never shone."[27] Thus, God was Just and Righteous in

---

[27] John Steinbeck, *The Winter of Our Discontent,* (London, England: Penguin Books, 1982) (Steinbeck 1982)

His judgement of this evil nation; who having tasted of His Goodness, rejected it.

> *For it is impossible for those who were once enlightened, and have tasted of the heavenly gift, and were made partakers of the Holy Ghost, And have tasted the good word of God, and the powers of the world to come, If they shall fall away, to renew them again unto repentance; seeing they crucify to themselves the Son of God afresh, and put him to an open shame. For the earth which drinketh in the rain that cometh oft upon it, and bringeth forth herbs meet for them by whom it is dressed, receiveth blessing from God: But that which beareth thorns and briers is rejected, and is nigh unto cursing; whose end is to be burned* (Hebrews 6:4-8).

AN EVIL NATION POISED FOR JUDGEMENT

Woe to the bloody city! it is all full of lies and robbery; the prey departeth not. (Nahum 3:1).

J. Vernon McGee parallels the city of Nineveh with that of our own United States, as to the direction we have turned.

> "What better description could you have even of our own country right now? I feel that we are given very few facts but a great deal of propaganda today. This is true not only Washington, D.C., and the news media but of all areas of our society.... The one thing that is needed today is the truth...We say that we live in a nation of law and order—but it hasn't been that. What an apt description this verse is of the United States! When I first

began to study to study this, I felt like asking Nahum, 'Are you talking about us?'"[28]

What was God's response?

Behold, I am against thee, saith the LORD of hosts; and I will discover thy skirts upon thy face, and I will shew the nations thy nakedness, and the kingdoms thy shame. And I will cast abominable filth upon thee, and make thee vile, and will set thee as a gazing stock (Nahum 3:5-6).

How sad it would be if after being founded on godly principles, our nation would reach the point in which God must say, "Behold, I am against thee." Yet, if the Christians of this nation do not stand as beacons of light shining into the darkness; the darkness will snuff out the light and we, as a nation, will stand judged by a Just and Righteous God.

A JUST AND RIGHTEOUS GOD'S OFFER OF GRACE

---

[28] McGee, *Thru the Bible*, 829

If my people, which are called by my name, shall humble themselves, and pray, and seek my face, and turn from their wicked ways; then will I hear from heaven, and will forgive their sin, and will heal their land (2 Chronicles 7:14)

If is such a big word. Have you prayed for our nation today? Have you laid your own sins before the cross of Jesus Christ in full repentance? Do you seek His Face each morning and throughout your day? Wake up dear Christian; before it is too late! Our greatest work is done on our knees. We must be the light shining into the darkness! That is our only hope. Remember God's warning to Cain?

"Why are you so angry?" the LORD asked Cain. "Why do you look so dejected?[7] *You will be accepted if you do what is right. But if you refuse to do what is right, then watch out! Sin is crouching at the door, eager to control you. But you must subdue it and be its master"* (Genesis 4:6-7, TLB).

Sin is crouching at the door of our nation. Every man and woman must answer and heed this warning of God. Will we accept His gift of grace, seek His face, and turn from our sin?

Cain did not heed the warning. Instead he killed his brother. What will we, as a nation do. God is calling to us.

THE LIES AND VIOLENCE

With so many lies encircling us from social media, mainstream media, politicians, and books; how can we know the truth? Remember,

Deceit is in the heart of them that imagine evil: but to the counsellors of peace is joy (Proverbs 12:20).

A good man out of the good treasure of his heart bringeth forth that which is good; and an evil man out of the evil treasure of his heart bringeth forth that which is evil: for of the abundance of the heart his mouth speaketh (Luke 6:45).

We must seek the truth through prayer, Bible study, and asking God for the wisdom to discern truth from fiction. If ever there was a time that we, the Christians in this nation should fast and pray for our nation, it is now! God has promised that if we seek His Wisdom and truth, He will give it to us freely!

If any of you lack wisdom, let him ask of God, that giveth to all men liberally, and upbraideth not; and it shall be given him (James 1:5).

Effie Darlene Barba

Chapter 15:

Awaken Christians, The Day of the Lord is Near

Awaken Christians, the day of the Lord draws near. As we turn from Nahum's judgement upon Nineveh, that wicked city, to now look at Zephaniah's prophecy; we cannot help but see how swift and complete will be the judgement upon this earth.

Zephaniah not only predicts the judgement upon Israel that would come; but also, the judgement that will ultimately come upon any nation who has turned their back on God. This small book, written by one of the minor prophets; presents glimpses of Jesus Christ who came to be the ultimate sacrifice for sin. He will return, bringing judgement upon this earth to all who have rejected the good news of the gospel message.

Zephaniah's words of warning came during the reign of Josiah, King of Judah. Although, Josiah lead the nation in revival; Zephaniah forewarns the people of the judgement that would come because of their once more turning their backs upon God. His prophecy also foretold of God's righteous, just judgement of all mankind one day.

> *The word of the LORD which came unto Zephaniah the son of Cushi, the son of Gedaliah, the son of Amariah, the son of Hizkiah, in the days of Josiah the son of Amon, king of Judah.*
>
> *I will utterly consume all things from off the land, saith the LORD.*
>
> *I will consume man and beast; I will consume the fowls of the heaven, and the fishes of the sea, and the stumbling blocks with the wicked: and I will cut off man from off the land, saith the LORD* (Zephaniah 1:1-3).

AWAKEN CHRISTIANS, GOD WILL JUDGE IDOLATRY

As Zephaniah begins to proclaim all those who will be judged in Judah and Jerusalem, he provides a list which we, as a nation; must consider. The list begins with idolatry.

Verse four of Chapter one states: *"I (God), will cut off the remnant of Baal from this place."* Idolatry is listed first in Zephaniah. This grave warning speaks even further into how a nation can fall into many forms of idol worship. Indeed, throughout the books of the Chronicles and Kings I and II; there is description of various evil Kings building altars to idols. The sad part noted: the people blindly followed their kings.

J. Vernon McGee points out in his commentary of this verse:

> The first step in a nation's decline is religious apostasy, a turning from the living and true God. The second step downward for a nation

is moral awfulness. The third step downward is political anarchy.[29]

Did anyone notice the remarks of Senator Feinstein in the confirmation hearings of Amy Coney Barrett, in which she refers to Christianity as a "dogma" that should never be allowed in a judge? Her remark was, "the dogma lives loudly in you and that is a concern."[30]

Dogmas are the core Christian claims.[31]

Shouldn't this bring concern for the Christians in this nation? Our core Christian claims are under attack by some in Congress.

Furthermore, look at the attack on morality. Condemned for taking a stand against sin, we are told to keep

---

[29] McGee, *Thru the Bible,* 864
[30] Senator Dianne Feinstein, "The Dogma Lives Loudly in You", *Washington Post.com,* accessed October 23, 2017, https://www.washingtonpost.com/video/politics/feinstein-the-dogma-lives-loudly-within-you-and-thats-a-concern/2017/09/07/04303fda-93cb-11e7-8482-8dc9a7af29f9_video.html (Feinstein 2017)
[31] James Beilby, *Thinking About Christian Apologetics,* (Downers Grove, IL: IVP Academic, 2011),19 (Beilby 2011)

quiet; because, our faith cannot enter our politics. Then, look at the anarchy on our streets and our University Campuses against anyone holding onto Christian Conservative Thought. Awaken, dear Christians and listen to the words of Zephaniah.

AWAKEN CHRISTIANS,

THE DAY OF THE LORD IS AT HAND

Zephaniah goes on to list those who should stand in fear of judgement.

1. Idolatry, particularly as it enters the realms of government and the people's hearts. (verse 4)

2. Those who worship in blackened robes, Satanic worship. (verse 4)

3. People that worship the stars; rather than, the creator of the stars. (verse 5)

4. Those who combined worshipping God with worshipping false Gods (verse 5).

5. People who have heard the gospel message and have turned their backs on God (verse 6)

6. Those who never sought the Lord, nor inquired of Him. (verse 6)

AWAKEN CHRISTIAN,

RECALL THE GOOD NEWS OF THE GOSPEL

Amid the warnings, Zephaniah foretells of Jesus Christ who will come to be the ultimate sacrifice, paying the price for our sins.

Hold thy peace at the presence of the Lord GOD: for the day of the LORD is at hand: for the LORD hath prepared a sacrifice, he hath bid his guests (Zephaniah 1:8).

Not only did Christ come to die on a cross for our sins; but, He will return one day to call for final judgement upon the earth. All those who know Him as Savior, Lord, and King will reign with Him that day. However, all who do not; will be cast into the lake of fire. When we remember God's Love; we must never forget His Righteousness and His Justice. With great mercy, grace and love, He provided a way of salvation. It is up to each of us to choose. Will we follow Him; accepting His gift, or will we reject it and seal our own fate for eternity.

> *We then, as workers together with him, beseech you also that ye receive not the grace of God in vain. (For he saith, I have heard thee in a time accepted, and in the day of salvation have I succoured thee: behold, now is the accepted time; behold, now is the day of salvation* (2 Corinthians 6:1-2).

And for our nation, the same is true. Awaken dear Christian, for now is the time to seek God's face, bow in prayer for our nation, and continue to spread the good news of the gospel. We must not be silenced in fear.

Chapter 16:
When Perfect Love and Judgement Meet, Where Are You?

Amid the rebuke and the pronouncement of judgement declared in Zephaniah, there reigns a theme of God's grace and perfect love toward the sinner. We see throughout the impending judgement and wrath of God, a thread of hope for mankind. When perfect love and judgement meet, where will you be standing?

> *Gather yourselves together, yea, gather together, O nation not desired; Before the decree bring forth, before the day pass as the chaff, before the fierce anger of the LORD come upon you, before the day of the LORD's anger come upon you. Seek ye the LORD, all ye meek of the earth, which have wrought his judgment; seek righteousness,*

seek meekness: it may be ye shall be hid in the day of the LORD's anger (Zephaniah 2:1-3).

Therein, we find our hope. Gather together all you sinners, deserving of God's wrath; and, seek the Lord. Seek His righteousness and seek meekness; so that, you may be hid in Him during the day of the Lord's anger. A righteous and just God must cry out against the sin and the evil of this world; otherwise, His Perfect Love is thwarted. There can be no semblance of perfect love, were there not judgment against the evil that destroys us from within.

LOVE DEMANDS JUSTICE

Even in judgment, God is still a God of love. And He judges because it is essential for Him to judge that which is evil. He does that because He must be true to Himself, and He could not be good to His creatures unless He did that. If God is going to permit sin throughout eternity, if God does not intend to judge sin, if you and I are going to have to wrestle with disease and with heartbreak and with disappointment and with sorrow throughout eternity, I cannot conceive that He is a God of love. But if you tell me that God is going to judge sin, that He is coming in with a mighty judgment, and that He is going to remove sin from His universe, I'm going to say "Hallelujah!" And I will believe He is a God of love.[32]

So, it remains; in a book proclaiming judgment, God's mercy and love is repeatedly proclaimed. His voice continues to call to each sinner, "Come and be cleansed by the blood of Christ Jesus." "It is a glorious, wonderful thing to be hidden in the cleft of the rock and to be covered by His wings."[2]

LOVE AND JUDGMENT MEET AS ONE

---

[32] McGee, *Thru the Bible,* 869

There is no place in all of history that declares this truth more clearly than the cross. There is a song that Avalon sings which perfectly portrays this. The lyrics are as follows:

"Where Joy And Sorrow Meet"

There's a place of quiet stillness 'tween the light and shadows reach
Where the hurting and the hopeless seek everlasting peace
Words of men and songs of angels whisper comfort bittersweet
Mending grief and life eternal where joy and sorrow meet

There is a place where hope remains
In crowns of thorns and crimson stains
And tears that fall on Jesus' feet
Where joy and sorrow meet

There's a place the lost surrender and the weary will retreat
Full of grace and mercy tender in times of unbelief
For the wounded there is healing, strength is given to the weak
Broken hearts find love redeeming where joy and sorrow meet

There's a place of thirst and hunger where the roots of faith grow deep
And there is rain and rolling thunder when the road is rough and steep
There is hope in desperation there is victory in defeat
At the cross of restoration where joy and sorrow meet[33]

---

[33] David James White, *Where Joy and Sorrow Meet,* Avalon Lyrics, accessed October 25, 2017, https://www.azlyrics.com/lyrics/avalon/wherejoyandsorrowmeet.html (White n.d.)

GOD'S LOVE AMID JUDGMENT

Although, Israel had sinned against God repeatedly, His covenantal love held fast. They would once more face judgment for their sin; because, God knew that sin would destroy them. Evil within their hearts would prevent them from ever knowing the sweetness of His presence among them. Sin would destroy their hearts; bringing evil and chaos within. Yet, even during their coming captivity; a remnant of faithful believers would emerge. From that remnant through the corridors of time, Jesus would come to die on the cross.

Last week, I allowed anger to enter my heart and wrote a letter I wish I could retrieve. God's judgement for my act would be deserved. My only hope, is that with a humbled heart; I will send an apology for that letter. I was wrong. Now, as I turn my heart in repentance to the one I most offended; I plead as did David.

For I acknowledge my transgressions: and my sin is ever before me. Against thee, thee only, have I sinned, and done this evil in thy sight: that thou mightest be justified when thou speakest, and be clear when thou judgest. (Psalm 51:3-4).

Now, with a humbled and contrite heart; I turn to God, seeking mercy. Whatever, the judgment may be; I accept. Then, I lay it all before the throne of Christ; where His mercy will carry me to where ever He leads today.

Seek ye the LORD, all ye meek of the earth, which have wrought his judgment; seek righteousness, seek meekness: it may be ye shall be hid in the day of the LORD's anger (Zephaniah 2:3).

Effie Darlene Barba

Chapter 17:

How to Know Love that Overcomes Rejection

The book of Zephaniah declares God's judgment on His people and upon all the nations of the world. In chapter one, we saw His pronouncement of judgment upon His people for their sins. Yet, amid the declaration of His just judgment; He foretells of the coming Messiah and the ultimate end of evil.

It is the story of a perfect love for a rebellious, head strong people who spend their time chasing after other lovers. A people whom He wooed with a perfect love; yet, repeatedly, they turned away from Him. He provided them fortress, manna, sweet water to drink; yet, they would turn away to seek after sin and worldly pleasure. They would build idols to other Gods, forsaking their one true love. Yet, God's love would rise above their rejection to love them still. With open arms, He waits from them to turn once more to seek Him.

Chapter two foretells of His judgment against the evil nations who tormented His chosen, as He foretells of the rise of Babylon to destroy the surrounding nations. Despite His rescuing them from their enemies; we know the next chapter of the story. They would once more turn their hearts away from Him and God would allow the Babylonians to take them captive. Through it all, God's love remained and reaches out to all who would accept that love. Amid all the pronouncements of judgment, Zephaniah is a story of God's undying love that calls forth and bids them come and rest in His arms of love.

GOD'S JUSTICE IN JUDGMENT

As we turn to chapter 3, we can hear the pleading voice of God; as He reminds His people of why His judgment had to come. Because their rebellious hearts and desire for sin brought chaos and evil into their land. Listen to His plea.

Woe to her that is filthy and polluted, to the oppressing city! She obeyed not the voice; she received not correction; she trusted not in the LORD; *she drew not near to her God. Her princes within her are roaring lions; her judges are evening wolves; they gnaw not the bones till the morrow. Her prophets are light and treacherous persons: her priests have polluted the sanctuary, they have done violence to the law.*

The just LORD *is in the midst thereof; he will not do iniquity: every morning doth he bring his judgment to light, he faileth not; but the unjust knoweth no shame. I have cut off the nations: their towers are desolate; I made their streets waste, that none passeth by: their cities are destroyed, so that there is no man, that there is none inhabitant. I said, Surely thou wilt fear me, thou wilt receive instruction; so their dwelling should not be cut off, howsoever I punished them: but they rose early, and corrupted all their doings* (Zephaniah 3:1-7).

Surely, after all I have done; you will hear my voice and heed my instructions. But, alas; they would turn to Him only for a moment and then once more go about their lives without a thought of the one who saved them.

WHAT ABOUT YOU AND ME? OR OUR NATION?

Is that not our story as well? How often we cry out to God when we face a crisis; only, to abandon Him when the crisis is over? Does your Bible lay closed on the bedside table; until, you are being attacked by the enemy? All too often that is the case. What about our nation? Have we not sat idly by while watching our nation turn against all Godly principles? Within our churches, we see the seeds of relativism rise; wherein, there is no moral authority or adherence to God's truth. He watches with great sorrow; for He knows outside of His presence; only chaos and evil exist. With great patience and love, He waits for me to turn once more to Him. Then with arms of love He draws me back into His arms to comfort me, when I turn to seek Him once more.

> *The LORD thy God in the midst of thee is mighty; he will save, he will rejoice over thee with joy; he will rest in his love, he will joy over thee with singing. I will gather them that are sorrowful for the solemn assembly, who are of thee, to whom the reproach of it was a burden. Behold, at that time I will undo all that afflict thee: and I will save her that halteth, and gather her that was driven out* (Zephaniah 3:17-19).

LOVE THAT OVERCOMES REJECTION

God stands with open arms, waiting for you and me to turn to seek Him. He waits patiently for our nation to turn their eyes once more to follow Him. Until we do, chaos and violence will continue to rise within. Outside of His presence there is no hope, no true love, no righteousness and no goodness. Then, why do we turn our backs upon the only one who can bring light into our darkness?

His love is big enough to forgive our moments of rejection; if only, we turn and seek Him. Despite our rebellious, adulterous hearts; He calls us to come home, so that He might wrap us in His arms around us and sing His love song of joy over us.

Chapter 18:

Could We as A Nation Be in Peril of God's Judgment?

Considering all that we have learned from Nahum, Habakkuk, and Zephaniah; what is the message for us today. God is love. Because of His love; He must remain true to Himself. Perfect love demands justice as well. Love always looks for the good of the beloved; therefore, true love cannot watch idly as the beloved wanders down pathways leading to their own destruction, chaos, pain, and sorrow.

God pleads with His Beloved to open their eyes to see their folly. He knows that joy, hope, and fullness of life are found in Him. He who created us so that we might be showered with His love, filled with His joy and share in His Magnificent Glory; knows our hearts can never be satisfied apart from Him. He paved the pathway and paid the ultimate price for us to know Him and the fulness of His Joy.

Yet, love cannot be forced upon the Beloved. He pleads with each of us and with our nation, to open our eyes to see and receive His perfect love. Desiring that which is perfect and beautiful for each of us. However, alas; many turn their backs and walk away. Believing that they can make a better path for themselves, they turn away and chase after idols. *Deceit is in the heart of them that imagine evil: but to the counsellors of peace is joy* (Proverbs 12:20).

We look around us today and realize how many declare truth as relative to how one perceives it; demanding that there cannot be any absolute truths. By thus, they deny the existence of God.

A FALLING NATION

We have seen the results of this vanity played out on the stages of our own nation. The death of morality, the rise in drug abuse, the ever-increasing violence, all are results of such vain ideologies leading to despair, anger and chaos. Zephaniah listed the reasons for which a nation can fall under the judgment of God and I think we should review those once more, considering how they apply to our nation today.

1. Idolatry, particularly as it enters the realms of government and the people's hearts. (verse 4)

2. Those who worship in blackened robes, Satanic worship. (verse 4)

3. People that worship the stars; rather than, the creator of the stars. (verse 5)

4. Those who combined worshipping God with worshipping false Gods (verse 5).

5. People who have heard the gospel message and have turned their backs on God (verse 6)

6. Those who never sought the Lord, nor inquired of Him. (verse 6)

IDOLATRY

Listed as one of the five woes in Habakkuk as well, Zephaniah begins with idolatry first. He refers to it both in the realms of false teachers within the churches and in government.

> *I will also stretch out mine hand upon Judah, and upon all the inhabitants of Jerusalem; and I will cut off the remnant of Baal from this place, and the name of the Chemarims with the priests* (Zephaniah 1:4).

J. Vernon McGee writes:

> The Scriptures, beginning with the Book of Judges, teach a philosophy of human government, which you find was true of God's people and of every nation. The first step in a nations decline is religious apostasy, a turning from the living and true God. The second

step downward is for a nation is moral awfulness. The third step downward is political anarchy. [34]

Anyone who looks at the news of today in the United States of America, must recognize that we have reached step three. It began within our churches, where arose so many that preached "the prosperity gospel", a one-sided God of love with no hint of his righteous, just nature, a removal of the cross from the pulpit in fear it would offend some; and the "Johnson Act" forbidding pastors from weighing in on politics. Then, as the nation began to worship the flesh rather than God, we removed the right to pray or read a Bible in school, legitimized abortion as a means of birth control, upheld sexual freedoms of all kinds, and deny the scientific legitimacy of gender. Furthermore, everyone's "pursuit of happiness" at whatever cost; has led to the breakdown of the

---

[34] McGee, *Thru the Bible*, 864

family. We worship money, power, and self; wherein, the end justifies the means.

> *A good man out of the good treasure of his heart bringeth forth that which is good; and an evil man out of the evil treasure of his heart bringeth forth that which is evil: for of the abundance of the heart his mouth speaketh* (Luke 6:45).

THOSE WHO WORSHIP IN BLACKENED ROBES

A quick google search of satanic worship would bring you to many churches which have grown out of a movement began by Anton LaVey in 1966. But, I daresay; their belief that we each are our own gods; mimics the new-age movement as well. Furthermore, although their robes are white in color; the message of the Ku Klux Klan is as black as these other. Within our midst lie many with blackened robes worshipping Satan; rather, than the one true God.

These were the Chemarims mentioned in Zephaniah 1:4. They were idolatrous priests who wore blackened robes. Yet, we find many who worship themselves; rather, than their Creator. All would fall within this category; particularly, those who teach others to follow them while even using scripture. One such teacher/ writer that comes to mind is Wayne Dyer. He passed away in 2015; however, his books and teachings live on; and all too often, have lead a lot of people to worship self, rather than God.

STAR WORSHIP

Many people follow astrology. It seems harmless to read your horoscope, seek astrological advice; however, it is a form of idol worship. God is in control of our destiny; not, the stars that He created.

And them that worship the host of heaven upon the housetops (Zephaniah 1:5).

There also are those who worship the stars as a means of guiding our lives through the study of the galaxies. One such famous star worshipper was the gentle, soft spoken Carl Sagan; who lead us on a journey of discovery through his video series, *"Cosmos."* He presented this with such beauty and grandeur that it would have been easy for those who did not recognize the truth, to begin a journey of star worship. God created the heavens, with all their beauty and wonder. Imagine how much more magnificently beautiful is He.

THOSE WHO COMBINED WORSHIPPING GOD WITH WORSHIPPING FALSE GODS

I addressed this somewhat under the title of idolatry; however, I do think it bares readdressing at this point.

them that worship and that swear by the LORD, and that swear by Malcham (Zephaniah 1:5).

Malcham is the name for Molech, the god of the Ammonites. It was a worship in which they sacrificed their children. The subtlety of it was that at the same time they professed to worship the living and true God… Molech was the god of the flesh. [35]

As a nation, do we not so worship the flesh and its sexual desires to the extent that we sacrifice our children? When we turn a blind eye to abortions, are we not sacrificing our children? We worship the right to control our own flesh; while, killing the innocent fetus.

PEOPLE WHO HAVE HEARD THE GOSPEL MESSAGE AND HAVE TURNED THEIR BACKS ON GOD

As a nation, we have spent many centuries with the freedom to teach and spread the gospel message; yet, we cannot help but see our religious freedoms be challenged every day. Those who desire to squelch our voices have

---

[35] McGee, *Thru the Bible*, 866

created a nation that has turned its back on God. We must awaken. We need missionaries and evangelists to rise within our own nation who will unashamedly preach the gospel of Christ to our nation.

THOSE WHO NEVER SOUGHT THE LORD, NOR INQUIRED OF HIM.

This is a grave warning to us as a people and as a nation. Judgment will come.

And them that are turned back from the LORD; and those that have not sought the LORD, nor enquired for him (Zephaniah 1:6).

Yet, now; God bids us to come and be saved. How long will He tarry? We do not know; but, today is the day of salvation. We can turn from all our follies and follow Him.

But without faith it is impossible to please him: for he that cometh to God must believe that he is, and that he is a rewarder of them that diligently seek him (Hebrews 11:6).

Are you seeking Him today? Are you reading His Word, the Bible? What about prayer: are you seeking His presence? Do you know Jesus Christ as your Savior and Lord? If not, I bid you come. He is the greatest treasure you will ever find, and He provides all your heart needs. In Him is life, abundant and full of joy.

Effie Darlene Barba

Chapter 19:

How to Overcome Divisions and Spread the Gospel

Consider the history, a people called of God would turn their backs upon the very one who had set them apart as His own. It would be a repeating story throughout the history of mankind. From the earliest rivalry between Cain and Abel, the story repeats itself; because deep within the hearts of all, sin crouches at our doorway.

Yet, amid all the conflicts, divisions, and battles created by prideful hearts; God has stood faithful to save aside a remnant. Those who would worship Him; and it is for their sakes, God would preserve His people. He provided for them and all who believe, a Savior who came and paid the ultimate price for all the sins. He would take upon Himself the sins of all the world; so, as to preserve a remnant on whom He could lavish His love and joy within their hearts.

The minor prophets: Nahum, Habakkuk, and Zephaniah continue this message of warning to all who turn their backs upon God. Beyond their warnings, they tell of hope for all who would worship God. Isaiah, who came before these minor prophets; spoke very clearly the warnings, while foreshadowing all of God's mercy, grace and love to save all who would follow Him.

DIVISIONS WITHIN THAT WEAKEN

"And if a house be divided against itself, that house cannot stand" (Mark 3:25).

Pride, jealously, and anger rang true throughout the history of God's people. Hearts rebelled; because of sin. This had been the case betwixt Esau and Jacob. Also, Jacob's sons carried on with jealously, pride and anger. Ten brothers burned with this anger, as they rose up and sold Joseph into slavery; while, tolerating their younger brother Benjamin. Ultimately, they were brought to their knees through famine, leading them to humble themselves before the one brother who truly worshipped God.

However, despite God having saved them from the famine, the Jewish nation remained in Egypt long enough to become enslaved by that empire and God would once more save them when they turned their hearts to worship Him.

That same division and rivalry continued down through the ages, ultimately leading to the nation of Israel being divided into two during the reign of Jeroboam I and Rehoboam. As a divided nation, the tribes were open to being destroyed by surrounding nations, who easily invaded. Indeed, there was a time when the tribes would battle each other. Throughout, there were those who would continue to worship God; a remnant, whose hearts called out to God.

ISAIAH 1: 2-4,9

> *Hear, O heavens, and give ear, O earth: for the LORD hath spoken, I have nourished and*

brought up children, and they have rebelled against me. The ox knoweth his owner, and the ass his master's crib: but Israel doth not know, my people doth not consider. Ah sinful nation, a people laden with iniquity, a seed of evildoers, children that are corrupters: they have forsaken the LORD, they have provoked the Holy One of Israel unto anger, they are gone away backward.

Except the LORD of hosts had left unto us a very small remnant, we should have been as Sodom, and we should have been like unto Gomorrah.

The nation would face peril and near extinction; because of their sin. However, a remnant would remain faithful; and through them, the Messiah would come to offer salvation to all who would accept this gift of Grace offered by Almighty God.

A CALL FOR DIVISIONS TO CEASE:

In fact, before the nation was sieged by Assyria; one king would call upon the entire nation to return to worship God. That King was Hezekiah. He rebuilt the temple, fortified the walls and called upon all the tribes to unite in worshipping God. He pleaded,

> *Now be ye not stiffnecked, as your fathers were, but yield yourselves unto the LORD, and enter into his sanctuary, which he hath sanctified for ever: and serve the LORD your God, that the fierceness of his wrath may turn away from you. For if ye turn again unto the LORD, your brethren and your children shall find compassion before them that lead them captive, so that they shall come again into this land: for the LORD your God is gracious and merciful, and will not turn away*

his face from you, if ye return unto him (2 Chronicles 30:8-9).

Alas, only a few came. The remainder stood in their pride. Assyria overtook them all; except, a small band held out in Jerusalem. They would also fall ultimately to the Babylonians; because, of their own rebellions against God, allowing the ideologies of universalism and idol worship to enter their nation. Apart from a brief revival under King Josiah, the nation; , turned against God.

DIVISIONS WITHIN OUR NATION

No nation can survive, if they allow divisions. We stand in a crossroads as a nation, divisions are rampant throughout. One is the division between universality of ideas versus populism. Will we allow the ideologies of universality to invade and destroy our nation? Or will we stand, as one nation under God? It is a question, we each must consider in our hearts. This wide division breaks down our nation.

Furthermore, we have allowed relativism to deny the existence of truth. We have allowed it into our churches, our schools and our own lives. God's truth is our only hope. The gift of salvation offered to all, we dare not speak; for fear of being rejected or ostracized. However, unless; we the remnant do not stand firm, holding fast to God: we will fall as well.

We do this first through prayer and Bible study, so that, we many know God. Then with loving, gracious kindness; we reach across the aisles of division to offer to all salvation. Much like King Hezekiah offered to all the tribes of Israel. Then, we continue in prayer and worship of God; pleading for our brothers and sisters to open their eyes and worship God.

OUR GREATEST COMMISSION

> *Master, which is the great commandment in the law? Jesus said unto him, Thou shalt love the Lord thy God with all thy heart, and with*

> *all thy soul, and with all thy mind. This is the first and great commandment. And the second is like unto it, Thou shalt love thy neighbour as thyself. On these two commandments hang all the law and the prophets* (Matthew 22:36-40).

It is not in anger that we shall overcome the divisions in this land. Rather, we must first seek God with all our hearts, minds and souls. Then, filled with His love and the desire to spread the gospel message; we will rise above the noise, to proclaim the truth. Some will come. We must be more concerned with the salvation of their souls, than with merely being right.

Chapter 20:

So, Dear Lord; What Do We Do Now?

Looking around us, we see injustice, pain, and sorrow. So, we cry out to God, "What do we do now?" We seek the Lord, wanting answers. Evil, hate, and violence appears to be winning. So, what can we do? What can I do? God's answer rings forth:

> *Learn to do well; seek judgment, relieve the oppressed, judge the fatherless, plead for the widow. Come now, and let us reason together, saith the LORD: though your sins be as scarlet, they shall be as white as snow; though they be red like crimson, they shall be as wool. If ye be willing and obedient, ye shall eat the good of the land* (Isaiah 1:18).

How sweet it is to know God's grace, that can wash us white as snow! We, who know the Lord, cling to that truth with all its promises. Holding Him close to our hearts, we know that He is our sweetest treasure. Yet, despite that truth; why do we hold Him hidden, secretively clinging onto our hope? Shouldn't we rather share His joy with everyone we meet? Why do we complacently march with the crowds, silent? Busy trying to be accepted, liked by those around us; yet, we become dim lights hidden. Too afraid to proclaim His truth, for fear that someone might be offended. The apostles faced imprisonment, ostracism, and angry mobs. Governmental leaders feared they would rise in power; therefore, became determined to squelch this Christian band of preachers. This is what Peter wrote.

I Peter 3:12-19

> *For the eyes of the Lord are over the righteous, and his ears are open unto their prayers: but the face of the Lord is against them that do evil. And who is he that will harm you, if ye be followers of that which is*

good? But and if ye suffer for righteousness' sake, happy are ye: and be not afraid of their terror, neither be troubled; But sanctify the Lord God in your hearts: and be ready always to give an answer to every man that asketh you a reason of the hope that is in you with meekness and fear:

Having a good conscience; that, whereas they speak evil of you, as of evildoers, they may be ashamed that falsely accuse your good conversation in Christ. For it is better, if the will of God be so, that ye suffer for well doing, than for evil doing. For Christ also hath once suffered for sins, the just for the unjust, that he might bring us to God, being put to death in the flesh, but quickened by the Spirit: By which also he went and preached unto the spirits in prison;

Effie Darlene Barba

OUR HIGHER CALLING: WHAT WE MUST DO!

We are to be always ready to give a reason for the hope that is in us. To defend the gospel of Jesus Christ to a world, hell bent on denying Him. However, how can they believe or inquire of our hope; when we look just as they?

When we worry and fret about the trivialities of our own lives, never displaying the peace and joy that is ours in Him; would anyone want to seek the God we say we trust? If our primary desires in life have become consecrated into our discovery of comfort, prosperity, popularity, and things in general; then, we who profess the name of Christ are indeed become impoverished. Only a relationship with God can fulfill all the longings of our hearts. Before we can be a light shining hope into our darkened world, we must know this and be satisfied in His presence with us.

What truly commends Christ as lovely in this world? It is NOT the one who proclaims that through faith they gained all the earthly pleasures. Rather, it is that dear soul; having lost everything this world can offer, whose eyes shine bright with joy, hope, and faith; because, they know Him. Willing to die, rather than to deny the one on whom their life depends.

PROSPERITY BREEDING COMPLACENCY

It is no wonder, our nation has forgotten; "In God, we trust". As a nation, we enjoy the blessings of prosperity. However, instead of praising God and turning to Him; our hearts become satisfied with counterfeit treasures. While at the same time, we forsake the only true treasure, the one who blessed us to begin with-God. Laying on the shelf somewhere in our homes, a Bible lays unopened. Our prayers of thanks before a Thanksgiving dinner, words only; unless, we see Him as our only hope, joy, and treasure.

It is no wonder, that the world does not see God as glorified in our lives, seeking to find Him. John Piper's ministries motto is: "God is most glorified in us when we are most satisfied in Him."[36] Satisfied in God: not our jobs, position in society, health, wealth, or prosperity. When we cling tight to the truth that in Him we live, breath, move and find our meaning. (Acts 17:28 paraphrased). As Paul preached before the Athenians he proclaimed this:

> *God that made the world and all things therein, seeing that he is Lord of heaven and earth, dwelleth not in temples made with hands; Neither is worshipped with men's hands, as though he needed any thing, seeing he giveth to all life, and breath, and all things* (Acts 17: 24-25).

---

[36] John Piper, *Taste and See: Savoring the Supremacy of God in All of Life,* (Colorado Springs, CO: Multnomah Publishers, 2005), 413.

(Piper, Taste and See: Savoring the Supremacy of God in All of Life 2005)

We must seek Him above all else. Yearning to know Him, arise early to read His Word. Seek Him in prayer, communing with Him. Then, as you discover Him; proclaim His Grace, Love, and Glory to the world through your life and your words. Then, and only then, will others see Him as Glorious and to be desired above all else. Our nation could be healed, if everyone who professes the name of Christ; would live a life reflective of His Joy, His Love, and His Glory within us. So, what are we waiting for?

Effie Darlene Barba

Bibliography

Beilby, James. *Thinking About Chrisitan Apologetics*. Downers Grove, IL: IVP Academic, 2011.

Calkins, Robert. *the Modern Message of the Minor Prophets*. New York: Harper and Brothers, 1947.

Edwards, Jonathan. "Concerning the Divine Decrees." In *The Works of Jonathan Edwards*. Edinburgh, Scotland: Banner of Truth, 1974.

Feinstein, Senator Dianne. "The Dogma Lives Loudly in You." *WashingtonPost.com*. September 9, 2017. https://www.washingtonpost.com/video/politics/feinsten-the-dogma-lives-loudly-within-you-and-thats-a-concern/2017/09/07/04303fda-93cb-11e7-8482-8dc9a7af29f9_video.html (accessed October 17, 2017).

Henry, Matthew. "Biblehub.com." *Matthew Henry Commentary: Habakkuk 2:5-14*. n.d. http://biblehub.com/habakkuk/2-5.htm (accessed October 4, 2017).

Johnson, Elliot. "Nahum." In *The Bible Knowledge Commentary: An Exposition of the Scriptures by Dallas Seminary Faculty: Old Testament*, by John and Roy Zuck eds. Walvoord, 1493-1504. Colorado Springs: CO: Victor, 2004.

Kapic, Kelly M. *Little Book for New Theologians*. Downers Grove, IL: IVP Academic, 2012.

King, Dr. Martin Luther, Jr. "Martin Luther King Quotes." *Movingtowardfreedom.com*. n.d. https://movingtowardsfreedom.com/tag/martin-luther-king-jr-quotes/ (accessed November 4, 2017).

McGee, J. Vernon. *Through the Bible with J. Vernon McGee: volume III Proverbs-Malachi.* Nashville, TN: Thomas Nelson, 1982.

Piper, John. *Taste and See: Savoring the Supremacy of God in All of Life.* Colorado Springs, CO: Multnomah Publishers, 2005.

—. "The Just Shall Live by Faith." *DesiringGod.org.* October 31, 1982. http://www.desiringgod.org/messages/the-just-shall-live-by-faith (accessed October 4, 2017).

Scott, Hillary, and and Bernie Herms Emily Weisband. "Thy Will Be Done,W.B.M. Music Corp." *www.air1.com.* 2016 . http://www.air1.com/music/artists/hillary-scott/songs/thy-will-lyrics.aspx (accessed September 25, 2017).

Stanley, Charles. *Charles Stanley's Handbook for Christian Living.* Nashville, TN: Thomas Nelson Publishers, 1996.

Starr, Penny. "Education Expert: Removing Bible, Prayer from Schools Has Caused a Decline." *CNSNews.com.* August 15, 2014. https://www.cnsnews.com/news/article/penny-starr/education-expert-removing-bible-prayer-public-schools-has-caused-decline (accessed September 29, 2017).

Steinbeck, John. *The Winter of Our Discontent.* London, England: Penguin Books, 1982.

Tada, Joni Eareckson. "Features and Bible Helps." In *Beyond Suffering Bible.* Carol Streams, IL: Tyndale House, 2016.

Tytler, Alexander. "Alexander Fraser Tytler: Quotable Quotes." *Goodread.com.* n.d. https://www.goodreads.com/quotes/108530-a-democracy-cannot-exist-as-a-permanent-form-of-government (accessed October 9, 2017).

White, David James. "Where Joy and Sorrow Meet, Avalon Lyrics." *www.azlyrics.com*. n.d. https://www.azlyrics.com/lyrics/avalon/wherejoyandsorrowmeet.html (accessed October 25, 2017).

Youssef, Michael. *The Barbarians are Here.* Franklin, TN: Worthy Publishing, 2017.

www.ingramcontent.com/pod-product-compliance
Lightning Source LLC
Chambersburg PA
CBHW071501040426
42444CB00008B/1443